TWO SISTERS

TWO SISTERS

BETRAYAL, LOVE AND RESISTANCE IN WARTIME FRANCE

ROSIE WHITEHOUSE

HURST & COMPANY, LONDON

First published in the United Kingdom in 2025 by
C. Hurst & Co. (Publishers) Ltd.,
New Wing, Somerset House, Strand, London WC2R 1LA
Text © Rosie Whitehouse, 2025

All rights reserved.

The right of Rosie Whitehouse to be identified as the author of this publication is asserted by her in accordance with the Copyright, Designs and Patents Act, 1988.

A Cataloguing-in-Publication data record for this book is available from the British Library.
ISBN: 9781805262718

www.hurstpublishers.com

Printed and bound in Great Britain by Bell & Bain Ltd, Glasgow

Cover design by Patrick Sullivan
Interior design by Kevin Ullrich
Picture credits appear on page 246

For Tim

CONTENTS

MAP OF FRANCE x
INTRODUCTION 1
MARION AND HUGUETTE MÜLLER'S FAMILY TREE 7

PART I: TWICE DISPOSSESSED

1 Berlin 11
2 Paris 23
3 The Exodus 34

PART II: THE SILENCE

4 The Revolution 45
5 In Love with the Resistance 57
6 The Invasion 66
7 The Conference 69

PART III: THE CHOICE

8 Two Boys 75
9 The Identity Card 84
10 The Reprieve 94

PART IV: A CHINK OF LIGHT

11 The Photographs 105
12 The Suitcase 117
13 A Month in Drancy 135

| 14 | The Rejected | 145 |
| 15 | The Killer | 157 |

PART V: THE SILENT VICTORY

16	Looking for Dr. Pétri	165
17	Jews with Guns	180
18	The Hotel	195
19	Sunday Morning in Val d'Isère	208

APPENDIX: THE PEOPLE IN THE WAGON	215
ACKNOWLEDGMENTS	225
AUTHOR'S STORY	227
BIBLIOGRAPHY	231
TOPICS AND QUESTIONS FOR DISCUSSION	235
INDEX	239
PICTURE CREDITS	246

"What would you have done? Most people turned a blind eye to the danger we were in, but a handful of people tried to help me. Why did they do that? Why did they stand up to evil?"

—Huguette Müller

MAP OF FRANCE

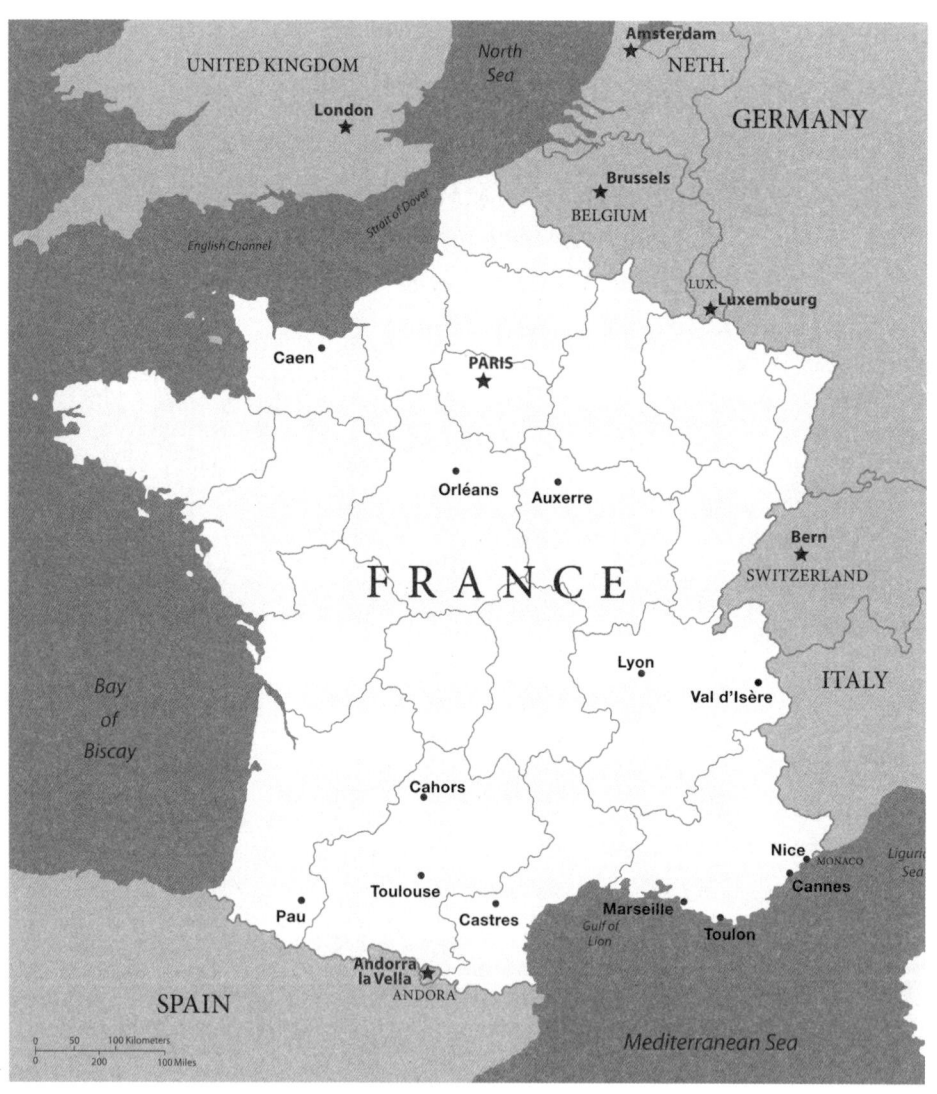

As the first snow began to fall in the winter of 1943, fifteen-year-old Huguette Müller and her older sister, Marion, fled from Lyon to hide out in Val d'Isère. Marion told her they were going on holiday in the Alps.

INTRODUCTION

In 1938, a young doctor, Frédéric Pétri, decided to join his friends in the remote French Alpine village of Val d'Isère. The group would turn it into one of the world's most famous winter resorts, but when the Germans occupied the valley in the autumn of 1943, its young men and women turned the best weapons they had against them—their skis. Adept at crisscrossing the region's mountain passes, Pétri and his colleagues set up a formidable but now forgotten resistance network.

As the first snow began to fall in the winter of 1943, fifteen-year-old Huguette Müller and her older sister Marion fled from Lyon to hide out in Val d'Isère. Marion told her they were going on holiday in the Alps. It was a lie. The Nazis had occupied southern France the year before, and in Lyon they had begun to intensify their hunt for Jews whom they were deporting to the death camps in the east. Their mother had just been arrested on the French Riviera and sent to the transit camp of Drancy. Although it would take years for the sisters to find out what had happened to her, she had already been gassed the moment she arrived in Auschwitz. The two sisters were all alone and had no one to turn to. Marion pinned their hopes of survival on the village. Not long before Christmas, disaster struck when Huguette, who could not ski, slipped and broke her leg.

INTRODUCTION

Dr. Pétri was called to help. He told Marion that her sister's leg was so badly injured, she needed to be moved to the hospital in the valley below. Marion knew that if she went with her sister to the hospital, she was likely to be caught by the Gestapo, who were on the lookout for suspicious people "holidaying" in the Alps. For Marion, it was the final betrayal. She punched the doctor in the face. Pétri did not flinch and continued calmly to explain that without the right medical care, her sister would end up with one leg shorter than the other. Terrified, Huguette cried out that it was better to limp than die. Pétri immediately realised that the two girls were Jewish. Without hesitating, he told Marion that he would look after Huguette himself in his own house. He warned Marion that it would be safer if she left the village immediately. He told her to return in six months, by which time Huguette's leg would be healed. In the meantime, she must not have any contact with them. Trusting the doctor, Marion fled.

If Dr. Pétri had not offered to care for Huguette, the scenarios that could have played out would have all been bleak. It is more than likely that the two sisters would have been arrested and would have followed their mother to Drancy and then Auschwitz.

Why a total stranger was prepared to risk his life for a teenage girl he had met just moments before has baffled Huguette all her life. Nor does she have any idea why her sister trusted the doctor. Marion did not like to talk about the war years and waved her hand dismissively whenever she was asked about it. Despite this, she returned to Val d'Isère numerous times after the war ended and brought her children and grandchildren with her.

※

In 2019, together with my husband Tim, I went to San Francisco, where Huguette has lived since 1948. Marion was Tim's mother. Huguette is his aunt. Just weeks before, Huguette, then aged

INTRODUCTION

ninety-one, had been knocked down by a car and had broken her leg for a second time. My husband felt time was running out to ask his aunt everything she could remember about the family and the war years. Marion had died in 2010 and we had never pushed her to tell us her story. She always kept her thoughts and feelings to herself. When Tim and I fell in love, there was a hullabaloo in the family because I was not Jewish, but Marion was always completely accepting of me. The only strong opinion I remember her voicing was her concern when we gave our five children identifiably Jewish first names. I often wondered what had happened to her during the war, but you do not ask your mother-in-law questions she does not want to answer.

Despite her injury, Huguette bustled about in the kitchen making coffee. Once she sat down, it did not take long to move the conversation to the winter of 1943. Not that having a conversation with Huguette would be that simple. She has been hard of hearing since birth and is now completely deaf. We had to write down everything on her iPad.

Huguette tried her best to answer my husband's questions, but she struggled to remember the doctor's name. "But he saved your life," said my youngest daughter, Evie, in disbelief. "When I returned to Val d'Isère in the 1970s to find him and thank him, it was too late," she replied. "His wife answered the door and told me he was dead. He was young and it was such a pity. I think he was called Pétri, but . . . I can't remember his full name, what can I do now?" The fog outside the window seemed only to compound the sense of confusion.

Out came the mobile phones and we soon discovered that the main roundabout in Val d'Isère is Place Frédéric Pétri. As soon as she saw this, Huguette confirmed immediately that the doctor's name was indeed Dr. Frédéric Pétri, and that he had lived in a large chalet with his mother and sister.

INTRODUCTION

"He was a very kind man," she added. "He carried me into the garden when the weather got better." She then said in a matter-of-fact tone, "That was that, when I went back, he was dead, so I could not say thank you. It was too late." Huguette is a practical person, who does not let the past haunt her, but she added, "I have never understood why he helped me."

There was a moment of silence before I suggested to Huguette that it was not too late to say thank you. Maybe I could find Pétri's family so she could thank them.

Huguette has always had a sense of what is right and what is wrong. She has fought in the courts to reclaim what was stolen from her family by the Nazis. Nor does she see things in black and white. After the war, Huguette became a teacher, and her second husband was a German whose father had been killed on the Russian front when he was a small child. It was completely in character that she immediately took up my offer to find the Pétri family.

Huguette then went on to explain: "Other people helped me too, in far smaller ways. I have never understood why they did that, either." She mentioned neighbours who had warned her that the Nazis were looking for her and a ticket collector who suspected that she was Jewish but turned a blind eye. She also wanted to know how, why, and where her mother had been picked up by the Nazis. Who was the strange man in a beret pushing a wheelbarrow who came the day after to tell her to pack a suitcase for her mother? Did he ever give it to her? Huguette was an elderly woman looking for closure, so I said I would try to find the answers to a myriad of questions that would explain how and why she had ended up in Val d'Isère.

Unlike Huguette, Marion was bitter and angry about what had happened in France during the war. She resented the indifference shown by the French far more than the outright hostility of the few, and always said that no one had ever offered her a helping

INTRODUCTION

hand. Marion rarely discussed her life before or during the war. She looked toward the future with a harsh sense of realism. It left us frightened of the past.

When I finally found Dr. Pétri's family, that would start to change. Huguette suggested that we put him forward to be recognised as Righteous Among Nations, an honour given by the State of Israel to non-Jews who risked their lives to save Jews during the Holocaust. The decision to award the honour is made by a committee at the Israeli Holocaust memorial, Yad Vashem. It is a complicated process. The application must be substantiated by personal testimonies and evidence of the danger that the Jewish person had found themselves in. This book grew out of that process, as I had to help explain to the committee who Huguette and Marion were and why they had been in danger.

I had a basic understanding of what had happened in France during the German occupation, but I did not know why Marion and Huguette were among those Jews in greatest danger of deportation to the death camps. The story that would emerge was dark and sinister. It was a tale of how the French State that they had put their trust in betrayed them and stripped them of their citizenship.

Nevertheless, Huguette, unlike Marion, did not want her story to be handed down to the next generation as a bleak nightmare, but instead, a small victory of good over evil. It would change the way we all looked at this painful chapter in the history of the family. The legacy that Huguette had decided to leave was far more challenging than a story of tyranny and fear.

It is not difficult to sympathise with victims and point the finger at wrongdoers. The truth is that Marion was right. Most bystanders drew into themselves and ignored what was happening to the Jews. But by deciding to search for the people who reached out to help her in the most frightening moments of her life, Huguette had asked a question that changed the prism through which we could look at the Holocaust. It was no longer simply a tale of persecutors and victims. It was more than just a Jewish story.

By shining the light on Dr. Pétri, a man who had a moral compass and clung to his values in the most difficult of circumstances, Huguette was asking: *What would you have done? Would you have turned a blind eye to evil and thought only of protecting your family and friends, or would you have stood by your principles?* Those questions turn the Holocaust into an ethical challenge for all humanity.

Trying to answer Huguette's simple question—*Why did people help me?*—would teach me that Nazis were not all-powerful and there was nothing predetermined in the Holocaust. In France, during World War II, public opinion mattered. The country was, until 1940, a democracy where people's individual voices made up the sum of the whole. People had a choice in the way they acted. Even the politicians in Vichy were able to choose to what extent they would collaborate with the Nazis.

This is a story in two parts. It is the tale of how a family was torn apart, but it is also the story of the dark years in French history in which two young women were betrayed by the country they put their trust in. The road that led to Dr. Pétri's door was, however, a long one that began in another country altogether, long before the sisters were born.

MARION AND HUGUETTE MÜLLER'S FAMILY TREE

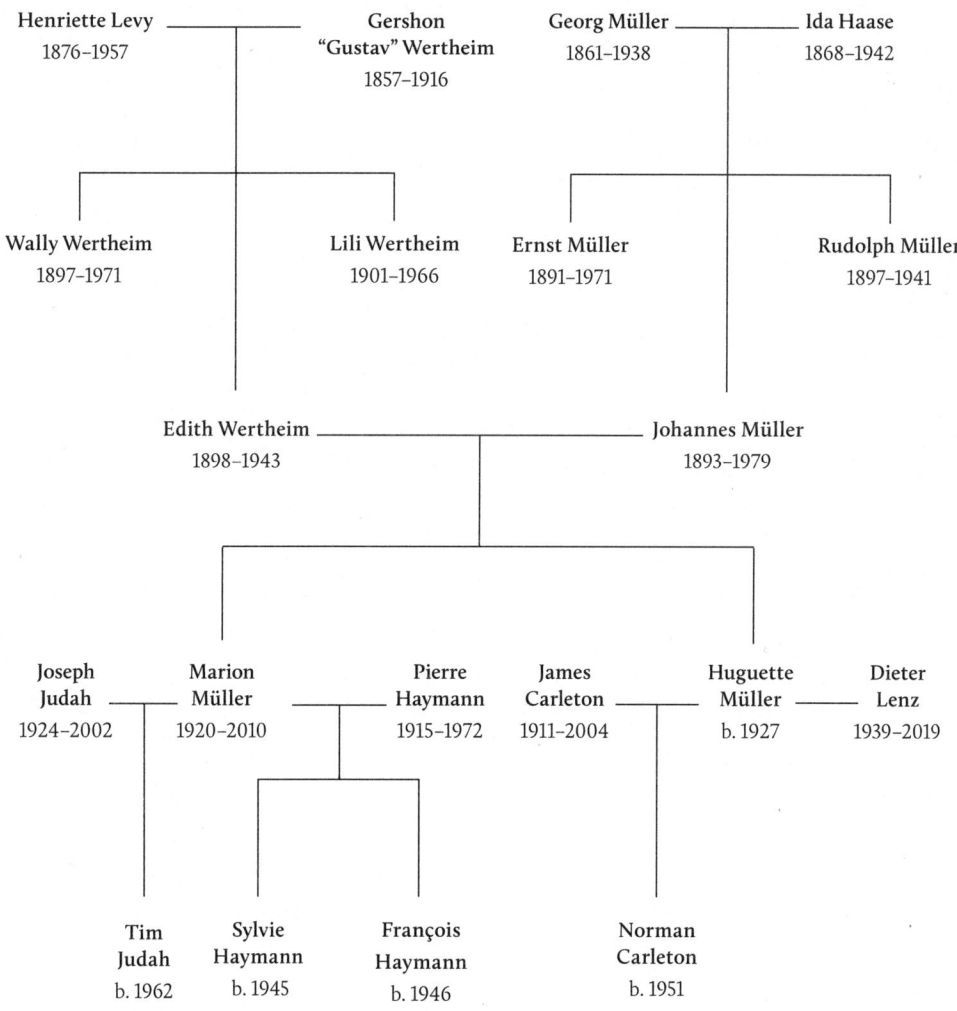

PART I
TWICE DISPOSSESSED

CHAPTER 1

Berlin

Before leaving San Francisco, I snapped a picture of Huguette and my husband next to the silver coffee set that once belonged to her mother. It now sits in pride of place on the sideboard in Huguette's elegant dining room. It is all she has left of the home she grew up in. It was a family reunion, full of smiles and laughter that hid the darkness.

Marion and Huguette lived two lives with their parents: one in Berlin and another in Paris, where after the war Marion married and raised a family. In 1948, Huguette left France for America, where she has remained ever since. Her son, Norman, is an American. Marion then lived her third life in London. She married Joe Judah, a Sephardic Jew who had been born into a wealthy Baghdadi Jewish family in Calcutta. My husband and I live in West London. Marion and Huguette grew up in a world that has disappeared in a city that none of us have any links to: Berlin. None of us speak German.

Marion was always adamant that she had no pictures of her parents and no mementos of the past. Yet, six months after she died, clearing out the musty box room in her basement, in an old grey

Edith Müller, c. 1919.

suitcase I found a tatty brown envelope that contained a handful of photographs. One was of a broody-looking man with dark eyes and a receding hairline. Another, in a tiny silver frame, was of a young woman in a white dress, her long hair tied up by a large white ribbon. They were Edith and Johannes Müller, Marion's parents. A jolt of panic shot through me. I felt like a thief stealing something Marion had tried to hide, but within moments I knew that I had misjudged her. Marion was not sentimental. If she had not wanted the pictures to be found, she would have simply thrown them away.

Huguette also claimed for years not to have any pictures from her childhood, but while we were in San Francisco, a collection of black-and-white photographs suddenly came to light. At the last minute, the story of their lives began to fall into place.

Among Huguette's photographs was a grainy black-and-white picture of her father in the German cavalry in 1915. Johannes was twenty-two years old at the time. He had just graduated from law

Johannes Müller. c. 1916.

school, but was now an officer in Berlin's Gardekorps. The division was deployed on both the Western and Eastern fronts, but in France—as early as September 1914—they had been forced to abandon their horses and dig trenches. In the photograph, Johannes is on horseback on an open plain that could possibly be in the east. The unit's records were destroyed during World War II, so it is impossible to pinpoint exactly where he saw action. What matters is that Huguette says that after just weeks at the front line he was seriously wounded and lost a foot. One of Marion's favourite stories was that her grandfather, Dr. Georg Müller, a renowned orthopedic surgeon who was attached to the Gardekorps medical team, went on horseback from one field hospital to another looking for his son. He would have known full well that on the front line, amputations were hurried, often botched procedures. Speed left painful nerves exposed and unsuitable stumps that could leave young men crippled. As Johannes lay in the hospital recovering, clumps of his hair began to fall out. It never grew back. He was awarded the Iron Cross 2nd Class. Another picture shows him recuperating in the garden with his parents. His mother, Ida, is dressed in white. The table is laid for tea. Johannes would spend the rest of his life with a prosthetic foot that he concealed by wearing boots.

Johannes had been an exchange student in Paris before the war. When he returned to his unit in spring 1916, he was sent to the front line to work as a translator in the Somme. Not long after, on July 1, the British and French offensive began one of the deadliest battles in history, the First Battle of the Somme. Anti-Semites in the German army and the Reichstag blamed the Jews for the enormous number of casualties and singled them out as shirkers. In October 1916, the Judenzählung, the army's census of Jewish soldiers, was ordered to assess their commitment to defending the Fatherland. The dead and the wounded, as well as the living, were to be counted. Johannes was a German nationalist and a deeply conservative man. The census was the first of a series of betrayals that would change the course of his life and drive him into exile. When the battle ended in November 1916, almost 450,000 German soldiers had been killed. Johannes was one of the lucky survivors.

Although the statistics compiled by the War Ministry failed to uncover any evidence that Jewish soldiers had evaded the front line, the findings were never made public. As the country collapsed in 1918, Jewish veterans faced accusations of cowardice and dereliction of duty. A myth rapidly gained ground that Germany had been stabbed in the back by a conspiracy of socialists and Jews.

By the time Johannes was demobilised, Berlin was in chaos; but more importantly, he had fallen in love with Edith Wertheim. The Spartacists, a radical group of communists, had called a general strike. Workers were demanding that factory owners hand over control to workers' councils. Before long the government called in the Freikorps, a militia made up of former soldiers to crush the rebellion. There was fierce fighting in the city centre and in the working-class section east of the city, where Edith's family owned a large textile factory, J Eichenberg AG. The business was already in crisis before the strike began. The market for J Eichenberg AG's clothes had almost dried up. It was impossible to fulfill what orders the company had as the supply chain had collapsed. Edith's mother, Henriette, was struggling to keep the business afloat. In 1916, at the height of the Battle of the Somme, her husband, Gustav, the company director, a round, jovial-looking man, had died of a heart attack. To keep control of the business, Henriette had forced the board of directors to appoint her in his place. J Eichenberg AG dominated the Wertheim's family life, sucking in everything and everybody into its world. Edith's older sister, Wally, was the company secretary who oversaw the day-to-day running of the business. Her husband was one of its directors and the chief accountant. Edith worked alongside her mother trying to secure business deals and negotiating with clients. When she married Johannes in 1919, Henriette gave her new son-in-law a seat on the board.

Marion was born in September 1920. Alongside the photographs of her parents that I discovered in Marion's basement was a picture of her sitting on her mother's lap, her eyes wide open and alert as if in anticipation of a surprise. She was about six months old, which meant it must have been taken in Berlin in the spring of 1921, just as her father organised the floatation of J Eichenberg AG on the stock market. At the same moment, the Allied Reparations Committee demanded that Germany pay 132 billion gold marks for the civilian damage caused during World War I. The economy could not cope. Three years later, as hyperinflation gripped the country, Marion would watch her mother barter a pair of gloves for a loaf of bread, almost magically conjuring up food to feed her daughter. Marion

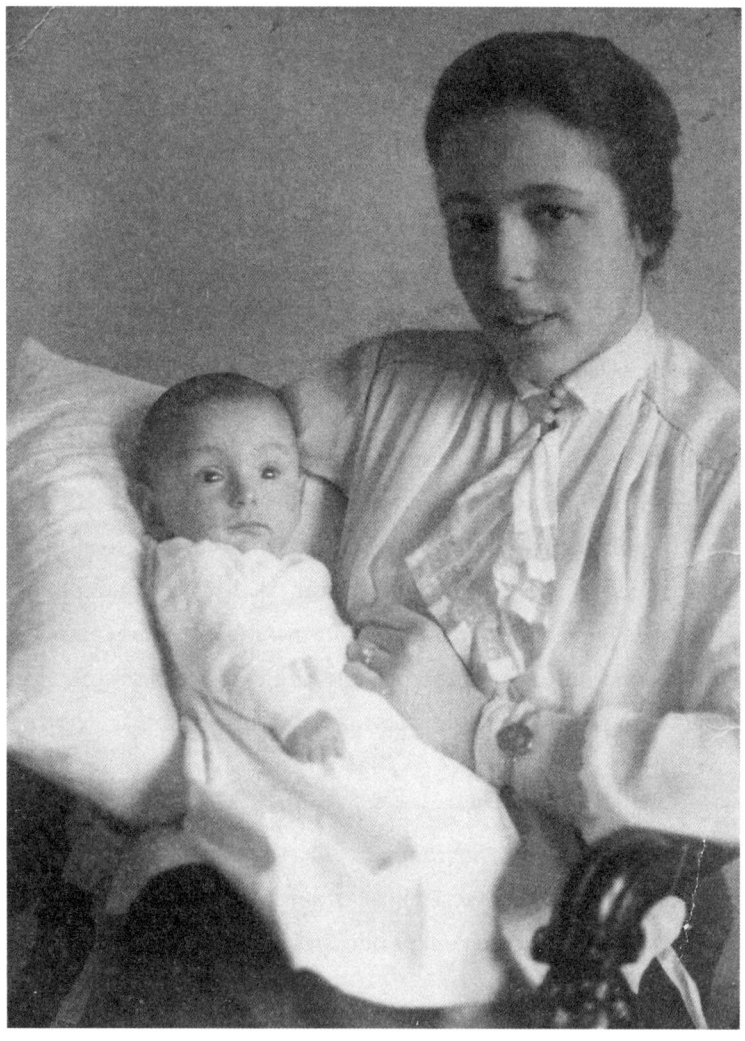

Edith and Marion, Berlin, 1921.

told this tiny snapshot of a tale with immense pride. She loved and admired her mother, but she hated her father, who had had a string of affairs. As soon as Marion was old enough, she spent the school holidays in the Art Nouveau factory learning how the company worked. She was taught how to operate the sewing machines on the factory floor and add up the accounts. Marion had a passion for clothes. She dressed immaculately and her hair was never out of place.

The only member of the Wertheim family to break free from the clutches of the business was Edith's younger sister, Lili. She became a nurse and embraced Berlin's wild cabaret nightlife. To my amazement, I discover that Lili's granddaughter, Tami, who now lives in Israel, has a collection of family photographs that will soon ping into my WhatsApp. Lili left Germany in 1934 and never returned. She must have taken them with her.

A picture of three sweet little girls in frilly dresses appears. The sisters—Wally, Edith, and Lili—grew up to be feisty teenagers, Tami says, and would drink their father's vodka and top the decanter up with water. They were an inseparable trio. Soon, postcards and holiday snaps follow. I presume no one dared to mention these photographs while Marion was alive.

By the time the German economy had stabilised in the mid-1920s, J Eichenberg AG was once again turning a handsome profit. In the 1920s, Berlin was the hub for the design and manufacture of luxury high-end ready-to-wear clothing known as *konfektion*. The *konfektion* industry was dominated by Jews, who employed a largely Jewish workforce. Henriette lavished her money on her daughters and her grandchildren, buying them gifts and paying for family holidays and day trips. Our cousin in Israel sends photographs of the sisters on holiday dressed in tight shorts playing with their children on the beach in Holland and walking in the mountains with their mother, Henriette.

In a more posed photograph, they sit on a row of chairs as their children ignore the camera and climb about on their laps. It must have been taken in Henriette's home in the affluent Berlin suburb of Dahlem. The villa had extensive gardens that ran down to the

The Wertheim sisters, Wally, Edith, and Lili, c. 1903.

lakeside and was the hub of family life. It was eventually requisitioned by the Nazis, who built a scientific institute on the grounds, which made Huguette's battle for restitution a legal nightmare that has never been resolved. Lili and her family lived with Henriette, where they had a floor of the house to themselves. Edith lived a stone's-throw away in a pretty, red-brick house with a pointed roof reminiscent of a gingerbread house.

By the time Huguette was born in 1927, Johannes and Edith were able to provide their daughters with everything they needed—and more. The family car was a cutting-edge American Chrysler that cost over $4,000, a small fortune in the 1920s. Weekends were spent on Berlin's lakes and in elegant cafés. Henriette was a hardheaded businesswoman. She had no time for domestic duties and employed a staff of servants who ran the house. She was, however, also a loving grandmother, who took her grandchildren for walks in the forest. She was passionate about nature and taught the children the names of all the trees. There were frequent trips to the cinema, which soon became Johannes's new passion. It seemed as if a new era had dawned, and that by the time Marion left school in 1938, she would be assured a seat on the board of directors at J Eichenberg AG.

Then the economic devastation of the 1929 Wall Street crash shook the foundations of the family business. Cutting costs and balancing the books consumed every minute of her parents' day, but the fall in the price of cotton did much to keep the company on an even keel. In 1931, it looked like J Eichenberg AG had weathered the storm, but the family fortune was now threatened by a political crisis that had erupted once the unemployment figures had hit a staggering four million.

After Hitler walked into the Reich Chancellery, in late January 1933, stormtroopers beat up Jews and marched through the streets condemning them as enemy aliens. Marion, now thirteen, was terrified. The multimillion-pound *konfection* clothing industry was one of the first to be singled out for Aryanisation. The April boycott of Jewish shops was an indication of what was to come for J Eichenberg AG. Bank loans and mortgages were suddenly withheld, and vandals attacked shops and factories across the city.

Non-Jewish friends and acquaintances, as well as clients, began to distance themselves.

At this moment Marion tried to join a scouting group. She was asked if her grandparents were Jews. When she went home and told her father, it was the last straw.

Marion sometimes claimed that until this point, she had no idea she was Jewish—her parents always had a Christmas tree, she said, as if that really proved anything. In Weimar Germany, Jews were more integrated into society than ever before, but even though they were a tiny minority—just 1 percent of the German population—there was still hostility to their presence. Johannes's parents had done everything they could to hide the fact that they were Jewish. His father had become a Protestant before World War I to advance his medical career. The conversion had happened just before Johannes's younger brother, Rudolph, was born. As a result, Rudolph's birth certificate says he was a Lutheran. Johannes and his older brother, Ernst, also adopted their father's new religious identity. It was, however, a "conversion" of convenience that did not fundamentally alter their Jewish identity and beliefs. Johannes's mother would slap Marion's hands if she waved them around too much when she talked. It was "far too Jewish," she warned her. The message was: *You are Jewish but keep it to yourself.*

One Sunday after lunch, prompted by her grandchildren's questions, Marion produced an envelope. After she had reheated the coffee that she had made for breakfast, she sat down and spread a series of pictures of her favourite cousin, Gunther, Lili's son, out on the table. One of them was taken in Palestine in the 1930s. It was proof that there was simply no way Marion did not know she was Jewish. In this tight-knit family, there was no way she could not have known that Lili and her husband were Zionists. It was a fundamental part of who she was. The Wertheims, although highly assimilated, celebrated Jewish High Days and holidays. Yet from her parents she had learned how to say one thing and think another. This symbiosis of external and internal self-perception would one day save her life.

Johannes and Edith were quick to see that there was no future for them in Germany. Step by step, the Nazis were destroying their livelihoods. They had no future in the place they called home—a country for which Johannes had put his life on the line and which they had thrown all their energy into rebuilding.

Henriette had no intention of giving in without a fight, and refused to leave Berlin. Edith's older sister, Wally, and her husband, who had no children, decided to stay with Henriette, but told Edith and Lili in no uncertain terms that they must flee the country for the sake of the children. There was a frantic scramble to find new lives elsewhere—anywhere—as the family was torn apart. Lili's husband left immediately for Palestine.

Within weeks, Johannes's father was barred from practising medicine. All his efforts to pretend he was not Jewish had been for nothing. For weeks his patients had failed to keep their appointments. If he stayed in Berlin, Georg would soon be a pauper. He had no choice but to leave. In the early summer, Johannes drove his parents to the Dutch border in the family Chrysler. It is not difficult to imagine the utter devastation and the deep betrayal Johannes must have felt as he stood alone and watched his parents walk across the frontier with all that they had been able to salvage of their lives. His older brother Ernst, who was also a doctor, left with his wife for the United States. Edith thought that they should follow him. Once family members left the country or made applications for visas at a foreign embassy, the entire family immediately came under surveillance and their letters were opened by Nazi officials. It was a terrifying development. In their house in Dahlem, there were weeks of serious arguments that Huguette has never forgotten. She says her mother was calm and never raised her voice, but the crisis that was swirling around them had pushed Edith and Johannes's marriage to the breaking point.

Johannes refused to listen to his wife, despite her desperate pleas. His skills were less transferable than his brother's. He did not speak English—how could he possibly get a job in America, he argued. He also had ambitions beyond commercial law and manufacturing. He was fluent in French. Spurned by one world, he was now drawn to the cosmopolitan and artistic life in the French capital. Furious, Edith continued to argue her case until he finally packed his suitcase and took the train to Paris. Johannes was adamant that this was where their future lay. Edith did not believe him, but he left her with no choice. Against her better judgement, she moved to France. One of Huguette's earliest memories is stepping down from the train onto the platform at the Gare de l'Est.

CHAPTER 2

Paris

On a blustery Sunday in October 2019, not long after we had seen Huguette in San Francisco, I meet my nephews, Marion's grandchildren, and their families for brunch just off rue du Faubourg Saint Honoré in the heart of Paris. At least half of the family still live in the city. My youngest daughter, Evie, has just started a master's degree at the École normale supérieure, one of France's *grandes écoles*. As soon as she arrives in the café, my great-nieces drag her off to view the cakes and biscuits on the buffet table.

I tell my nephews that Huguette has asked me to find Dr. Pétri's family and that Huguette would like to ask Yad Vashem if he could be recognised as Righteous Among Nations. I add that I want to finally find out exactly what happened to Marion and Huguette during the war. They look skeptical and the conversation moves on, but just before the bill arrives, one of them pulls out his cell phone and shows me a document he had found online. It is the ruling on a case Huguette had submitted to the Claims Resolution Tribunal from 2004 to gain access to funds in her father's Swiss bank account, which had been closed in 1938. The tribunal valued the account at 10,375 Swiss francs, which she was awarded. It lists two addresses where Edith and Johannes lived in Paris during the 1930s. When my nephew tells me he has had this for years, I am flabbergasted that he did not tell us before. Then, as I queue up to pay the cashier, I realise we are all the same: we have bits of information but are tentative about sharing what we know as it might not be the right moment to bring it up. This story has a grip on us all—just how tight it is I am only just beginning to realise. Many Holocaust survivors say that they were reluctant to tell their families about their experiences because they did not want to upset them. They wanted to keep their children distanced from the sadness and the pain. As I am about to discover with Granny Marion, it was not that simple. The bill paid, I return to the brunch table and during a round of hugs and kisses, I ask my nephew to AirDrop me the document. Outside in the street I tell Evie to jump in the car.

In the summer of 1933, Johannes rented an apartment at 43 rue de la Ferme in the fashionable suburb of Neuilly-sur-Seine in the west of Paris. In the autumn drizzle, we drive across the city through modern underpasses and large roundabouts until we arrive in the smart suburbs that surround the Bois de Boulogne. On rue de la Ferme, there are a few unassuming pre-war two-story houses dotted along the street, but at number 43, there is a block of modern flats. Totally deflated, I sit and look at the building from the car window. At first, it seems that modern reality has erased the past I am looking for, but as we sit there in the pouring rain, I realise that the building does not matter—what counts are the memories that stand out in Huguette's mind.

Johannes arrived in Paris a changed man. Betrayed by his country, he rejected everything that linked him to Germany. It was as if a switch had flicked off in his head. Overnight he assumed a new identity and from now on went by the name Jean Paul. He turned from a German nationalist into a French patriot. Invigorated, he found himself in charge of his family's future. No longer forced to listen to his mother-in-law, he gave a string of orders to his wife and daughters, who were told to follow his lead and reinvent themselves. From now on, the family would go to church, only speak French, and embrace everything that Paris had to offer. Johannes, however, had not told Edith the truth. He was not only captivated by France—he was terrified of it.

He had studied in France in the wake of the Dreyfus affair, which had divided the country into two hostile camps. In 1894, Captain Alfred Dreyfus, a Jewish officer from Alsace, had been wrongly accused of treason and sent to a penal colony. He was finally pardoned in 1906, by which time the case had poisoned French politics and set the tone for the decades to come. The anti-Semitism that surrounded the affair convinced journalist Theodor Herzl that there was no future for the Jews in Europe and turned many Jews toward Zionism. The hatred and violence that would burst into the open in 1940 were already swirling around Huguette and Marion's family as they moved into their new home.

In the 1920s, France had welcomed immigrants, as World War I had led to a shortage of labour and conscripts, but after the Great Depression hit, politicians decided to impose immigration restrictions. As unemployment soared, a hatred of foreigners, who could possibly steal their jobs, rippled through all layers of society. In the ultra-conservative press, the 55,000 refugees who had fled to France from Germany morphed into millions in the editorials.

On the right, there was a deeply entrenched dislike of foreigners. Since the nineteenth-century French conservatives had been fearful that immigration would dilute French culture, and for many, the most dangerous immigrants of all were the Jews. The Jewish community in France was divided not only within itself, but also in the eyes of the general public. Fully assimilated French citizens, referred to as *Israélites*, accounted for just over half of the 350,000 Jews living in the country. They were integrated into all levels of society. The remaining 140,000 Jews were of foreign origin. Some of those recent immigrants had become French nationals, but the majority had not. They were widely regarded with scorn by both French Jews and the rest of the public. Anti-Semitism was far from marginalised in France and was embraced by some of the country's leading intellectuals. One of the most important political movements in the Third Republic was the fiercely anti-Semitic Action française, whose chief ideologue, Charles Maurras, advocated a form of ethnic nationalism, La France aux Français—France for the French. A dislike of foreigners was a core part of conservative French politics.

Johannes therefore ordered his daughters to never tell anyone they were Jewish, and forced his family to hide who they really were years before World War II erupted. The dismissive wave of Marion's hand was not a reluctance to talk, but a deliberate tactic to evade prying questions. Johannes left his wife and daughters with no choice. They had to become as French as they possibly could in their tastes, in the clothes they wore, and even in the food they ate. It was no longer a game of "conversions" of convenience. It was the cleverest thing he ever did and, in 1943, it would save his daughters' lives.

Johannes instilled in Marion a passion for all things French that would never leave her. Marion even spoke English with a French accent, unlike Huguette, who has always had a German accent when she speaks English. She was determined to hand on her French nationality to her son from her second marriage in Britain, Tim, and our five children. She took them to Paris regularly and was delighted when we sent them to the French Lycée in London.

Yet at the time, Johannes's insistence that the family speak French and French alone must have felt unimaginably cruel. Huguette says her mother struggled, making endless grammatical mistakes, and had a terrible accent. Neither she nor Marion could speak a word of French, either. After Marion died, I found the little red Silvine notebooks she had used while learning English after she moved to London. She had written not just random words, but whole sentences in English—neatly, in pencil, like lines to be learned for a part in a play. She must have done the same thing in her bedroom on rue de la Ferme. Huguette, who was just five years old, withdrew into herself and for almost a year after arriving in France refused to say a single word.

At her father's insistence, Huguette was baptised and says she can still remember the trickle of water on her forehead. "My father was very strict and always said that we were Catholic," she says, "but I always knew that I was Jewish, and it wasn't true." I think that it must have been Edith who reminded her daughters who they really were. It was a wise move, because many of those who had become totally assimilated were caught by surprise when the Nazis arrived in France.

For Edith, the shock of being forced to flee her home must have rocked her to the core. The familiarity and purpose of her daily life that revolved around the factory had disappeared. She had lost her career and the support of her family. The dynamics of her relationship with her husband had changed beyond recognition. Unable to have a proper conversation, it was virtually impossible for her to make friends. Johannes continued to have a string of affairs and dispatched Marion to a Catholic boarding school in Nantes on the Atlantic coast. Edith must have been unbearably lonely, stuck at home with a little daughter who for months refused to speak to her.

Huguette before the war, c. 1935.

As she practised her French by translating the front pages, Edith must have slowly realised that the country she had sought refuge in had a dark and dangerous side. From now on, she would follow the news religiously. Marion was just like her, and spent hours reading the papers. Just before Christmas 1933, the headlines were grabbed by a scandal that linked government ministers in the financial dealings of a conman named Alexandre Stavisky, who was also a Polish-Jewish immigrant. The story was picked up by *L'Action française*, the newspaper of the far-right group of the same name. The paper accused not only the government of being rotten to the core and manipulated by Jews, but also disparaged as illegitimate the entire political system of the Third Republic that had been set up after the collapse of the Second Empire during the 1870 Franco-Prussian War. The crisis escalated when Stavisky was found dead. The extreme right claimed he had been murdered to stop him from divulging secrets. The political atmosphere was explosive, and throughout January 1934 there were violent clashes on the streets of Paris between the police and right-wing vigilantes, who were convinced a left-wing coup was in the offing. This kind of street violence had been common in Berlin and must have made Edith extremely nervous.

On the freezing cold night of February 6, 1934, a mob gathered in Place de la Concorde, determined to storm across the bridge over the Seine, break into the Chamber of Deputies, and topple the government. They attacked the police with cobblestones and railings from the nearby gardens in the Tuileries, slashing the bellies of their horses with razor blades attached to canes. The police opened fire, killing a dozen people and wounding hundreds. The night was a baptism of fire for the intellectual and political generation who came of age in the 1930s. Among them was Louis Darquier de Pellepoix, who would eventually become France's wartime Commissioner-General for Jewish Affairs. De Pellepoix was wounded in the riot. While he was recovering in the hospital, a friend gave him a copy of *The Protocols of the Elders of Zion*, the fraudulent anti-Semitic pamphlet. Inspired, he went into politics and became a local councilor in Paris.

Conspiracy theories abounded as politics moved onto the street. The conservatives drew closer to the extreme right, whose agenda began slowly to become state policy. Strict visa restrictions were reinstated, and in a dangerous precedent of legal exclusion, foreign-born citizens were banned from taking up careers in law and medicine for up to ten years after they had been naturalised. It was an uncanny mirror image of what had driven the family from Berlin. Alarmed, politicians on the left united as the Popular Front. When they took power in 1936 under the Jewish socialist Léon Blum, the floodgates of right-wing paranoia swung wide open. Thousands of anti-Semitic leaflets, funded by the German government, were handed out in the streets of Paris, and Jews were attacked as they went about their daily lives. A violent political subculture developed, and La Cagoule, a French fascist-orientated group, carried out a terror campaign of murders and bomb plots designed to look like a communist insurrection.

It was against this backdrop that, after months of silence, Huguette began to talk. The first thing she told the family was that she wanted to change her name. At this point, she was still known by the name her parents had chosen for her—Inge Margot—but she was being bullied at school. The children in her class could not pronounce Inge, and called her *singe*, the French word for *monkey*—she was not sure if it was on purpose. In the hope it might improve her chances at fitting in, she decided to name herself after a girl named Huguette, who had the best marks in the class. The plan failed. School was a constant struggle and source of anxiety.

In Palestine, Edith's sister's life was no easier. Lili and her husband had opened a shop selling imported children's clothes on King George Street in Jerusalem. In 1936, she received the devastating news that her sister's shop had been burned to the ground in an Arab arson attack. A British magistrate had ruled that they were not covered by insurance. Although the letters disappeared in the chaos of war, I have no doubt Lili wrote to tell her sister that they had lost everything and that they had decided to seek refuge in America. Edith would never see her again.

The news from Germany was equally alarming. In 1935, the Nuremberg Laws stripped Jews of their citizenship, but it was a slow process that took years to implement. Nevertheless, in March 1938, just before the family lost their German passports—and under the 1927 French law that eased the naturalisation rules—Johannes and Edith became French. Despite all his anxieties, Johannes must have felt his dreams were finally coming true. He was now not only a French citizen, but he had also become part of the dynamic cultural life he so admired. As a film producer and distributor, he was behind a string of box office hits, among them the *Roi de Camargue*, a "Camembert western" set in the wild marshes of the Camargue; and *La Symphonie des brigands*. He was successful enough to be able to employ Marion, who had just left school and was dreaming of becoming an actress. The boardroom of J Eichenberg AG belonged in another universe. In the summer of 1938, the family moved into a smart apartment at 59 rue de Miromesnil in the chic 8th arrondissement, an elegant street that runs from Métro Villiers to the Elysée Palace.

The international situation was, however, deteriorating rapidly. Paris was tense. In September, Hitler demanded that the Sudetenland, a border area of Czechoslovakia containing an ethnic German majority, was handed over to Germany. War seemed imminent. Anti-Jewish demonstrations that cut across the political divide broke out. Whipped up by the press, many French believed that the Jews were warmongers. Jewish property was attacked and people who simply looked foreign were beaten up in the street.

Things looked like they could not get any worse until in November, when a seventeen-year-old Jewish teenager, Herschel Grynszpan, walked into the German Embassy in Paris and shot the third secretary five times in the stomach. Grynszpan was an illegal immigrant, and his parents were among 12,000 Polish-Jewish citizens living in Germany who had just been expelled and dumped across the border in Poland. He was trying to bring attention to their plight, but their problems were soon overshadowed. In the Reich, the assassination sparked a frenzy of government-backed violence known as Kristallnacht. Synagogues were burned to the ground, Jewish shops attacked, and 30,000 Jews arrested. The Nazis claimed that Grynszpan was an agent of an international Jewish conspiracy that intended to provoke a war between France and Germany. It stoked the anxieties of the appeasers, and the new conservative French government—which had replaced Blum's Popular Front—tightened their surveillance of foreigners, leaving them liable to internment.

Then, in February 1939, came the devastating news that Henriette had been forced to sell J Eichenberg AG at a bargain-basement price to an Aryan company. It was unbelievable that the company had survived this long. The Nazis hated the Jewish ready-to-wear fashion industry so much that they even outlawed the use of the word *konfektion*. Under their new owners, the factory would produce Wehrmacht uniforms and clothes for concentration camp prisoners. The story of this extraordinary Jewish fashion business would disappear from memory; when the war came to an end, the factory in Prenzlauer Berg would find itself in East Berlin behind the Berlin Wall. Huguette and her cousin, Lili's daughter, would eventually manage to reclaim the building after the fall of communism.

Wally and her husband fled to London. Henriette, with the help of the Red Cross, sought refuge in Sweden. Stoically, she accepted her lot and became a refugee in the house of a Polish-Jewish family who lived in Sweden. There, for the first time in her life, she had to learn how to cook and clean the house to pay for her lodging.

On the brink of war, the family who had lived in Germany for hundreds of years had lost everything and the ties that bound them together had been blown apart. For Edith and Johannes, everything hung on their new life in France.

CHAPTER 3

The Exodus

At five o'clock in the morning on May 10, 1940, the high-pitched wail of the sirens on the Eiffel Tower cut through the air. Edith and Johannes ran to the window and looked up at the empty sky in fear. The Germans had invaded Belgium, Holland, and Luxembourg. Three days later came the terrifying news that the Wehrmacht had broken through the thick forests of the Ardennes.

Bedraggled refugees were soon seen on the streets of Paris pushing carts and prams loaded with suitcases and pots and pans. The smell of burning paper wafted in through the French windows of the sitting room on rue de Miromesnil as officials in the ministries burned files and documents. Rumours flew around—all of them contradictory—as the German army pushed toward the Channel ports to take the fight to the British army stranded on the beaches of Dunkirk. Life in Paris, however, went on with a veneer of normality until just before lunch on June 3, when a low buzzing sound could be heard through Edith's kitchen window. It grew louder until it became a persistent, menacing drone. There was a rattle of anti-aircraft guns, and then came the deep, reverberating echo of explosions. The Citroën armaments factory on Quai de Javel was blown to pieces. The tension inside the apartment must have been palpable. Marion was in the south of France working for her father, and only twelve-year-old Huguette was at home. Even if her parents hid their fear from her, there must have been arguments and recriminations behind closed doors.

The following day, when Edith tuned in to listen to the evening radio bulletin, she would have heard the frightening news that the German army had arrived at the small market town of Roye in the Somme, just seventy miles north of Paris. Johannes had been north of Roye on the front line in World War I, and, when he finally came home from seeing his mistress, he must have assured his wife that the German advance would be stopped. There was no way that the Germans could break through the French defences, he told her. He had seen that with his own eyes. Yet, the next morning, a column of weary men from the 109th Infantry was already retreating from Roye across the flat exposed beet fields, as the screaming whine of a Stuka dive cut through the air. The planes strafed the column. Bullets ripped through the soldiers' haversacks, scattering tubes of toothpaste, toilet paper, and letters from home in pools of blood.

The soldiers of the 109th were all reservists—bakers, bankers, shopkeepers, hairdressers, and waiters—who had endured weeks of fierce fighting. Among them was Captain Pierre Haymann, an auburn-haired twenty-five-year-old who had been, until the mobilisation, a traveling salesman. Within months, Marion would fall in love with Pierre. The days that followed the fall of Roye would convince him that he and his men had been betrayed by collaborators and leave him determined to continue the fight against the Nazis. It would change Marion's life forever and set her on a course that would eventually help her save her sister's life.

In the early evening of June 6, the soldiers of the 109th had pulled back to the tiny, deserted village of Crapeaumesnil. The families who lived there had already joined the long columns of refugees fleeing south. To the north, the fires in Roye lit up the night sky. The commander of the 109th, Colonel Edmond Marchand, wrote a detailed account of the days that followed. Although their supply lines were cut and there was nothing to eat, he says, his men remained confident that they could stop the German advance. At dawn, the soldiers began to dig trenches in front of the village. Two walled farms sit on either side of the narrow road that leads into it as if it is a small fortress. On either side of the road there are two walled farms, behind which the houses, village hall, and the church fan out in a triangle. To the east are woods and copses. In 1940, young saplings had grown up beside the trunks of the trees that had been blown to pieces in the battles over twenty years before. To the west of the village is a walled cemetery that provided perfect cover from enemy fire.

For four hours in an eerie silence the soldiers watched the road that runs north in a straight line across the fields toward Roye. German reconnaissance planes crisscrossed the clear blue sky, but there was no sign of the French air force. Then the Wehrmacht began to advance across the fields. A series of blinding explosions shook the earth as thirty tanks suddenly appeared. A hail of bullets rained down on the trenches. Marchand's men held off the attack as the cries of the German wounded boosted their morale. The evening papers in Paris reported that the front line was holding, but under what Marchand called a "deluge of fire," the Germans surged through the French defences at the entrance to the village. Pierre Haymann was soon fighting for his life through cottages where dirty dishes lay abandoned on the tables and in gardens where the washing was still hanging out to dry, now covered in clods of earth thrown up by the shells.

The narrative set in the months after the battle of Crapeaumesnil was that the defeatist French army simply collapsed. The stereotypes of stupid generals and cowardly soldiers still endure, but Marchand's account makes it clear his men were far from demoralised and showed extreme courage as they regrouped in the woods to the east of the village. There is no hint of an inevitable disaster as the rest of the front line held steady. There was no rout. The Germans were too exhausted to take advantage of the gains they had made—but the window of opportunity to resupply and regroup was missed, and at dawn the German attack began again.

On rue de Miromesnil, the sound of distant artillery fire could be heard through the window. Parisians besieged the banks to withdraw their savings, and Huguette rushed home excitedly to tell her mother that school had closed early for the summer holidays. It was ominous news. The Nazis were on the doorstep. It was a catastrophe that no one had expected. In the city, terror spread like wildfire. As the world fell apart for a second time, Edith took down her suitcase. She must have slipped a supply of cash into the lining before she carefully collected her jewelry. Trying to remain calm, she rolled her nylon stockings and folded her clothes. She had far more to fear than the possible bombing raids and street-to-street fighting that terrified most Parisians. When she went to the newspaper kiosk to buy the evening papers, the reports said that Marchand's men were still holding the line, and on the ground in Crapeaumesnil, the German bombardment was indeed dying down.

Marchand's men had not eaten for forty-eight hours and had no supplies of ammunition or reserves to back them up. Nevertheless, he says they were determined to fight on when, out of the blue, they received orders to retreat. His men, he says bitterly, were forced to "voluntarily" leave the front line and pull back to Pont-Sainte-Maxence, thirty miles to the south.

It takes an hour to drive from Crapeaumesnil to the riverside town of Pont-Sainte-Maxence. The road runs across high exposed fields and then dips down suddenly into wooded valleys. Exhausted, Pierre must have looked up in dread as the road rose up yet again in front of him. There were just six hours of nightfall to provide cover, but the retreat was held up by the crowds of civilians fleeing south. Army trucks and military ambulances that had run out of petrol lay abandoned on the side of the road. It was only in the late afternoon that Pierre and his men finally arrived at the banks of the Oise, but before they could cross the river, German planes swooped down and destroyed the bridge. Now the only way across was over a tiny lock farther downstream. It was too weak to support the artillery, which they dumped in the river. Colonel Marchand received orders to hold the line at the Oise, but was then immediately told to withdraw to Senlis, nine miles to the south.

In Paris, at the southern end of rue de Miromesnil, the president's official residence, the Elysée Palace, was silent. The government had fled. At the stations, there was widespread panic as people on overcrowded platforms fought to get on the last trains leaving the city. There was simply not enough room for everyone. People were left stranded on the platforms, and thousands had no choice but to make their way southward on foot. There were no officials left to organise the exodus. It was every man for himself.

⚜

I park the car opposite 59 rue de Miromesnil. Edith's home is an elegant building with black wrought-iron balconies. The sturdy, grand wooden doorway is firmly locked. Without the entry code, I cannot even glimpse inside the stairwell. As I stand in the street, I can imagine Edith and Johannes frantically running backward and forward across the road as they pack the car. Huguette is already in the back seat. Johannes lifts his wife's leather suitcase into the boot as she dashes upstairs to grab her winter coat and her furs. She locks the door for one last time. The clatter of her smart heels echoes as she walks quickly down the hallway. The large wooden door clicks shut behind her. At just forty-two, Edith was five years younger than Johannes.

As they drove out of Paris, in Senlis, the 109th were trying to hold the front line at yet another river—this time, by the dark brown waters of the Nonette. Yet again, the Germans failed to break through the lines and cross the river, but on June 12, the 109th were ordered to retreat eastward around the capital. The French government, now in Tours, had declared Paris an open city. There would be no resistance. Paris had fallen. The unthinkable had happened.

As the sun rose on June 14, two trucks of German soldiers drove slowly from Porte de la Villette along Avenue de Flandres to the city centre. The capital was now under Nazi control. The Loire was to be the next front line. For Johannes, the race was on to cross the river, which is wide and dangerous, before the bridges were blown up.

Six million people had abandoned their homes. Laden down with pets and children, they pushed bicycles and prams crammed with all that was left of their previous lives. Huguette had never seen so many cars in her life. In their car, the family crawled along the road, in second gear, barely covering thirty-five miles a day. Towns and villages along the way were deserted, the doors and windows of the shops were boarded up. There was nothing to eat. Abandoned trucks and cars lay in ditches, their doors flung open. Exhausted people sat by the roadside in despair next to hedgerows full of lupins and bright yellow gorse. Nazi planes repeatedly swooped down, bombing the columns of refugees. Bodies were left scattered along the roadside. There was no one to help the wounded.

As the Germans pushed relentlessly on toward the Atlantic coast, Johannes and Edith finally arrived in Pau, just fifty miles from the Spanish border. The Italians had opened a second front on the Riviera, and now the only way out of France was through Spain. But there was still time to try to escape.

As Pierre and the surviving soldiers of the 109th marched into Jargeau, west of Orléans, eighty-four-year-old Marshal Philippe Pétain, the new head of state, was broadcasting to the nation in his thin metallic voice. "With a broken heart," he said, "I tell you fighting must cease." Some of the soldiers vomited in shock. Others, like Pierre, felt angry, bitter, and betrayed. When Pierre had received his call-up papers, France had been one of the most powerful empires in the world. It was impossible to believe the country had been defeated. Most ordinary people, however, welcomed the armistice that was signed on June 22. They simply wanted the fighting to stop and they put their trust in Philippe Pétain, the World War I commander at the Battle of Verdun. Pétain was a national hero admired across the political spectrum. The people trusted him and expected him to protect them. Pétain appeared to have saved France's honour and prevented an all-out occupation. The French believed that Pétain himself was the "shield" that would protect them from the German occupiers, while Charles de Gaulle, fighting abroad on the battlefields, was the "sword." It is an idea that has never entirely faded away. So strong was their belief in the Marshal that crowds threatened soldiers who refused to lay down their arms. At Vierzon, bystanders killed a tank officer who tried to hold the bridge over the Cher. Pierre and his men were among the two million soldiers who now found themselves prisoners of war. They were taken to a camp, Frontstalag 153, just outside Jargeau.

But there was one man, General Charles de Gaulle, who rejected the armistice. He fled to London with a handful of supporters, where on the BBC he called for the French to carry on the fight. Although few heard his broadcast, it heralded the next phase in the battle for France, in which Marion and Pierre would find themselves on the front line.

PART II
THE SILENCE

CHAPTER 4

The Revolution

Pau was teeming with confused, distraught, and disorientated refugees. As they had fled from Paris, Edith and Johannes had been united by the need to get as far away from the Nazis as they possibly could—but that unity did not last. Huguette remembers that in the hotel in Pau, her parents had bitter arguments about what they should do next. She says that they knew no one and that her father's mistress was nowhere to be seen, which only stoked the tension created by his infidelities as they were stuck alone in a pokey hotel bedroom.

Huguette was once again without her older sister to support her. After the invasion, Marion had found herself unemployed as her father's film ventures in the south of France collapsed. Befriended by one of the stars of his "Camembert westerns," a French Roma actress and painter named Tela Tchaï, the two women picked cherries in the Var to make ends meet. They became close friends, and when the going got tough, Marion would stay with Tela in Grimaud, not far from St. Tropez.

In Pau, Edith insisted that they had to get out of France as fast as they could. They had to try to get to Lisbon, and from there, to the United States. Johannes pointed out that there were long queues at the border and visas for Portugal were difficult to obtain. Edith argued that it was still possible, even at this eleventh hour—but Johannes refused to listen to her. His heart was elsewhere. The desire to see his mistress, Lucette, ten years younger than his wife, stopped him from making any attempt to leave.

France was a dangerous place. The country had not just been defeated, but was now in the middle of a revolution. On July 9, parliament granted Marshal Pétain extraordinary powers and dissolved the Third Republic. The État français, the French State, which took its place, was anti-democratic and xenophobic. The new government, based in the spa town of Vichy, believed the Third Republic had been undermined by Jews, foreigners, communists, and freemasons, who all needed to be surgically excised from society. *Liberté, Egalité, Fraternité* was replaced with a new state slogan, *Travail, Famille, Patrie*—Work, Family, Homeland. *Patrie* meant France for the French, *La France aux Français*. The new state was not one that would protect the Müller family.

The spearhead of the revolution was a new legal commission, the Commission de révision des naturalisations, which was set up to review all naturalisations granted since 1927. The commission's job was to strip unworthy foreigners of their citizenship. In the reality of 1940, foreigners were synonymous with Jews. Few people raised objections, and the press, now muzzled, did not protest. Oddly, in many classic accounts of the history of Vichy France, the commission is mentioned only in passing, but its establishment was a crucial development that put Edith, Johannes, and their daughters in the line of fire. Just how dangerous the new commission could be was made clear when the newspapers reported that naturalisations granted under the Popular Front government, like the Müllers, would be the first to be reviewed. As the new law affected over a million people, and the commission was only due to start work in September, Johannes must have calculated that he would have time to come up with a plan. After all, it had taken the Nazis three years to strip the family of their German citizenship. Johannes's immediate priority was to get out of Pau, which seemed to him a perilous place to stay.

German troops had arrived in Bayonne, just seventy miles to the west, on June 27. The armistice had divided France in two and a demarcation line now ran between the Occupied and the Free zones. There was, however, no guarantee that Pau would remain in the Free Zone. It was possible that the Germans would take control of the entire Spanish border. Police on the streets were already stopping people and checking their papers. German Jews without French passports were being arrested and taken to an internment camp in nearby Gurs. The Müllers' papers stated quite clearly that they had been born in Berlin. Johannes decided to move the family to Cannes, where he had contacts in the film industry. He hoped he could find work in the Victorine studios in nearby Nice.

For some people the war closed doors, but for others it offered new opportunities. Johannes was one of them. Yet again, in the middle of a crisis, he seized the moment to change his life. In Cannes, he took an apartment for himself and Lucette, and rented a small house for Edith and Huguette. Marion was soon reunited with her mother.

As Edith put down her suitcase in her new bedroom, she must have found it hard to control her anger. As she hung her clothes in the wardrobe, the fearful realisation that she and her daughters were trapped must have mingled with the disbelief that her husband had made no effort to rescue them.

Huguette was just twelve years old. She was still a child, and has only happy memories of the first summer she spent in Cannes. It was like a holiday, she recalls. It is a credit to her mother that she remembers it that way. Edith must have done everything she could to shield her from the reality of the situation. Along the Mediterranean coast the atmosphere was poisonous, and the economy was dangerously unstable. Not long after Johannes and Edith arrived in Cannes, there was a run on the banks. The French had repelled the Italian invasion, but Mussolini's ongoing territorial claims on Nice increased the nationalist fervour. In scenes reminiscent of Kristallnacht, the destruction of Jewish property orchestrated in the Reich in 1938, Jewish shop windows were smashed in Nice and Marseille. The stones thrown through them had scraps of paper attached upon which were scrawled "The National Revolution has begun" and "Punish the Jews." *L'Eclaireur*, the main daily on the Côte d'Azur, published a series of articles in September 1940 that referred to the problem of foreign refugees, a euphemism for Jews. Similar articles appeared in *L'Opinion du Sud-Est*. Most French decided it was wise to trust the government and get used to the new order, which looked set to stay. The fall of France had not just been a French defeat, but had also been a disaster for the Allies. An invasion of Britain seemed imminent.

※

In 1944, the xenophobic language that filled the newspapers was pushed into the shadows, but it has never faded away. Since the 1980s, it has been the basis of the political programme put forward by the right-wing leader of the National Front, Jean-Marie Le Pen. After the war, *L'Action française* became *Aspects de la France*, and in 1947, Le Pen began his political career selling the newspaper. Le Pen once ran a recording company that sold records of Nazi songs and

Hitler's speeches. He is also an Islamophobe, an anti-Semite, and a Holocaust denier. He has run for president five times; his daughter, Marine Le Pen, as leader of the National Rally—the successor party of the National Front—has run three times.

In 2002, I arrived in Cannes the day after Le Pen senior had made it into the final round of the presidential election. Among the policies he was advocating was that people whose grandparents were not born in France should be stripped of their citizenship. Among the millions of other French citizens who would have been affected were my five children, crammed into the back of the car. As we drove past his party's campaign headquarters, the flags were flying and loud patriotic music was playing. My eldest son was so upset and angry that I decided to leave the coast and find a remote hotel in the countryside—but there was no escape. Le Pen was all over the news: on the television, in the restaurant, and in the bar. The debate about who is French and who is not has only intensified since the terrorist attacks in Paris in 2015. When Le Pen's memoir was published in 2018, it was an instant bestseller. Obviously, not everyone who bought his book was a supporter of the far right, but they were interested in finding out about the man and his ideas.

♣

When Edith went to do her shopping in the market, she would have walked past Cannes's enormous late-nineteenth-century town hall that dominates the old port. It was here that the National Revolution that was set on driving her and her daughters out of the country was being rolled out. In August 1940, a memorandum was sent to all departmental *préfets* in the Free Zone asking them to bring suspicious cases to the denaturalisation commission's attention. To identify the whereabouts of people they needed to review, the *préfets* turned to local mayors and the police, who relied on the busybodies and gossips whose loose tongues—with the help of a small gratuity—turned them into informers. A woman with a strong foreign accent living alone with children had now become suspicious.

Marion had lost her job as her father's company collapsed in the wake of the invasion. She had to find work and went to Lyon, where she had school friends and hoped to find a job. Edith and Huguette, left alone, were increasingly vulnerable. Edith had to be extremely careful. To find friendship and companionship was now an incredibly risky thing to do. She was more alone than she had ever been.

Until the German invasion, ships sailed across the world from Cannes. As Edith walked along the portside, she must have tried as hard as she could to think of a way to join Lili, who was now in California, or Wally, in London. In New York and Washington, American Jews lobbied for visas and raised funds to help celebrity writers and artists, but there were limits to what they could achieve. The Emergency Rescue Committee managed to acquire 200 visas for prominent anti-Nazi intellectuals to be brought to the United States, but there was no hope of escape for a middle-aged housewife like Edith. Washington had recognised the Vichy regime, and the State Department had no desire to upset diplomatic relations. Nor was there any pressure from public opinion in America to loosen immigration restrictions.

Huguette says that her mother tried to hide her fears, but it soon became impossible for her to do so. On October 3, Vichy passed the first of a series of anti-Semitic laws, the Statut des Juifs, which defined a Jew as someone with three Jewish grandparents. The new law made Jews second-class citizens and banned them from working in a range of professions, including the civil service and the media. The entertainment clause was especially harsh, as the film industry was blamed for undermining the nation's morals. To carry on working, you needed a professional identity card that would prove you were not Jewish. For Johannes, another career had come to an end. The next day, a new law gave *préfets* the power to detain "foreigners of the Jewish race in special camps" or put them under "house arrest."

※

When Huguette asked me to help her find the family of the young doctor, Frédéric Pétri, I had imagined that I was embarking on historical research that had little contemporary resonance. The story of the dark years of the Nazi occupation has periodically returned to the national debate in France, and, as I began to piece together Marion and Huguette's story, it became a hot political topic once again.

In 2022, the right-wing TV star and pundit Éric Zemmour campaigned in the presidential election. One of his controversial beliefs is that Pétain and his government did everything they could to protect French Jews. It is a fact that foreign-born Jews made up the majority of those who were deported from France during the Holocaust. And it's also true that from day one, politicians and civil servants in Vichy were unsure how the public would react to measures taken against Jews who were French nationals and had been for generations, and so tried to prevent their deportation— but that does not mean that they protected them. The Statut des Juifs was not only aimed at foreign Jews. It hit French citizens just as hard. The teachers, lawyers, and university professors who all lost their jobs were mostly French Jews. Zemmour chooses to ignore the fact that a copy of the draft of the Statut des Juifs, discovered in 2010 and now held in the archives at the Mémorial de la Shoah in Paris, was marked up in pencil by Pétain. It shows how closely he was involved in every step of drawing up the Statut, which began: *"Nous Maréchal de France, chef de l'Etat français"* ("We, the Marshal of France, head of the French State"). At the bottom is his signature.

The paragraph intended to spare Jews born as French citizens from the prohibitions is crossed out in pencil—much like an item might be removed from a shopping list. Despite the claims he made after the war, Pétain had no intention in his domestic policy of distinguishing between French Jews and Jews who had been born as foreign nationals. Although some French supported the statutes, most people simply ignored the new law, as it had nothing to do with them. The Catholic Church, which supported Pétain's conservative government, was silent.

When Edith went to buy the newspapers in December 1940, the front pages were dominated by Pétain's tour of Provence. The pictures looked as if he was on a victory parade. On the Côte d'Azur, he was regarded as a local hero because he owned a holiday home in Villeneuve-Loubet, just north of Antibes. The reports she read described the huge flag-waving crowds that greeted him. There was little sign that anyone had any sympathy for the Jews, like Johannes and Marion, who had just lost their jobs; or the foreign-born nationals like the Müllers, whose cases would be reassessed by the new denaturalisation commission.

Along the Riviera, thousands flocked to join the new Légion française des combattants. The Légion brought together veterans from World War I and was one of the great mass movements of Vichy, with over a million members. Its heartland was in Alpes-Maritimes, where it soon had over 50,000 members—one in five of the population. It was led by Joseph Darnand, who had been a member of the violent insurrectionist group La Cagoule. At its launch, he told the 8,000-strong crowd that the Légion needed "true French patriots to replace wops, Jews, and foreigners. . . . We must drive out the false French, who have led this country to ruin." They were soon seen marching around the streets of Cannes.

In the New Year, Huguette began the school day by singing the Marshal's praises:

> *Maréchal, nous voilà!*
> *Devant toi, le sauveur de la France*
> *Nous jurons, nous les gars*
> *De servir et de suivre tes pas*
>
> Maréchal, here we are!
> Before you, the saviour of France
> We swear, us lads
> To serve and follow your steps

But the Marshal did not care for children like Huguette. Nor, it seems, did her father.

At the moment she needed him the most, Johannes simply washed his hands of his family. The Riviera was cold and rainy. It had nothing to tempt him to stay. In late October, Johannes returned to Paris with Lucette. Marion never forgave him for abandoning her mother. Huguette says if he had stayed, he would have been caught by the Nazis as well and is surprisingly not bitter that he left her and her mother alone.

Huguette was unaware that no sooner had her father left Cannes than the first list of denaturalisations was published in the *Journal officiel*, the government gazette. The 445 names ran over eight and a half pages. A week later, it was posted in the town hall and the local court. Edith must have waited in fear until it appeared in the local newspaper a fortnight later. Naturalisation was granted to family units and, as a result, denaturalisation was a patriarchal affair. I can feel the relief Edith must have felt when the name Müller, Johannes was not on the list.

As winter drew in, Cannes became increasingly dark and gloomy. The casino was closed, and on the seafront promenade, in the luxury hotels, well-heeled Jewish exiles from Paris waited in fear of what would happen next. In boardinghouses near the station, impoverished, unemployed Jews crowded into the cheapest rooms. The locals resented them all. They envied those with money to burn and looked down on those who found themselves on hard times. In December, the temperature plummeted, and heavy snow covered the boats in the harbour. Huguette remembers throwing snowballs, but at home it was cold and even though Edith tried to remain cheerful, she must have been lonely and resentful. Not that Johannes had completely disappeared. Huguette says that her father wrote to her mother and she knew where he lived. She has no idea if he sent Edith money, but says her mother sold some jewelry and a fur coat.

But even if you had money, there were shortages of absolutely everything. There was no detergent and no soap. Washing clothes took more time than ever, and Edith's hands were red and raw from the scrubbing. The joie de vivre of the casinos and grand hotels had been a fragile illusion. Alpes-Maritimes was barren and poor. Meat, potatoes, flour, milk, cheese, and eggs are all still imported from richer parts of France, but the dislocations of war and shortages across the country nearly severed all supplies as the first winter of the occupation set in. Hunger drew people into themselves and hardened their hearts to the plight of others. Huguette recalls being constantly hungry, but it was the silence that Marion would never forget, the silence of rejection and disinterest.

♣

Despite her age, Huguette is sharp and quick-witted, but there are many things she cannot recall about her childhood. The trauma of what was yet to happen has blocked them out of her memory. She cannot remember the address where she lived with her mother, nor the name of the school she attended.

In Cannes's Municipal Archives in a once-elegant villa, I search for documents that might mention Edith's name and her address. There are masses of letters and official papers that detail exactly how many eggs and grams of meat and flour people were allocated, but there is no list of who was entitled to coupons, although one must have once existed. The archivists suggest that I look at files from the local schools. By now, Huguette was in secondary school, but the school register for the boys' lycée is the only one that has survived. All that remains from the war years at the girls' school is a series of class photos. I struggle to recognise Huguette in any of them. The archivist then mentions that there was also a Catholic girls' school, and, although there is nothing in the archive relating to it, I assume that Johannes must have enrolled her there before he left.

The archivist soon realises that the family were Jewish and, sensing my frustration, digs out all files that they do have for the period that relate to Jewish matters. A tiny pile is placed in front of me. In one of the binders is a magazine, *Je vous hais* (*I Hate You*). The cover boasts that inside there are 150 pages of "absolute sensation." I open it up and go cold inside. It is so diabolically racist that I am momentarily frozen in panic. My instinct is to close it as quickly as possible, but I force myself to read page after page that describe how the Jews are spies and part of an international conspiracy, as well as thieves and prostitutes. The magazine cost 10 francs. From the moment Vichy repealed the 1939 decree that banned anti-Semitic publications, the magazine stands were piled high with publications like this, illustrated with horrible caricatures of Jews with hook noses. They terrified Huguette, who stood and stared at them as people casually picked them up, handed over their money, and took them home.

Huguette loved the cinema just like her father. For a weekly treat, Edith took her to see the latest releases, but she has never forgotten the fear she felt when in the spring of 1941 posters went up advertising the Nazi blockbuster *Le Juif Süss* (in German, *Jud Süß*). It is one of the most anti-Semitic films ever made. In France, it was seen by an estimated one million people. Also drawing the crowds was a so-called documentary on the Rothschild dynasty, *Le Juif éternel* (*Der ewige Jude*), during which at regular intervals, rats spilled onto the screen as if invading the theatre. The first thing Huguette did when she gave birth to her son was to check that he did not have a hooked nose like the Jews in the propaganda posters.

CHAPTER 5

In Love with the Resistance

In the autumn of 1940, Marion arrived in Lyon. She had to find a job and stand on her own two feet. Lyon was the most important city in the Free Zone and there were plenty of job opportunities. Not only was Lyon an industrial town, whose industry the Nazis intended to use to boost the German war effort, but after the armistice, many newspapers and organisations had decamped from Paris and set up shop in the city.

Marion went to stay with an old friend from school. She had just turned twenty and was a beautiful young woman whose brown curly hair framed her face. Marion had a radiant smile and a love of life and could no doubt have charmed her way into any job. What she did I do not know, but it was probably dull in comparison with the turn her life was about to take.

One evening in the freezing winter of 1940, Marion went to a party, where her friend introduced her to Pierre Haymann, the brave auburn-haired twenty-five-year-old reservist who had fought to defend the village of Crapeaumesnil. Pierre had made a daring escape from the prisoner of war camp in Jargeau just before the prisoners in the camp were moved to Germany. He swept Marion off her feet, and in a whirlwind romance, they fell in love—and joined the Resistance.

Pierre had made his way from Jargeau across the acres of fields and forests until he reached the demarcation line. There he crossed illegally, probably under the cover of darkness. He then went to Lyon where his sister lived with her husband. Pierre was determined to carry on the fight. In Lyon, he quickly made friends with other soldiers who had also managed to escape from the Germans.

Like many of those who were the first to join the Resistance, Pierre was Jewish, and his father, Albert, had fought in the trenches in World War I. The Haymanns hailed from Alsace but had lived in Paris since the mid-nineteenth century. His father ran a small department store in the 12th arrondissement, not far from the Gare de Lyon. Middle-class, assimilated, and secular, they were die-hard patriots committed to the Republic. The recognition that the Jewish army captain Alfred Dreyfus had been wrongly accused of being a German spy in 1894 had only made that commitment deeper. For Pierre, it was not only the Nazis who were the enemy, but the new French government as well. Pierre joined the Resistance to fight for the restitution of the France he believed in, where he had had equal rights with all other French citizens.

Marion was young and impetuous. Without her father to tell her what she could and could not do, she was free to do as she wished. Before long, Marion had moved in with Pierre. Together they began a new life in a dangerous world of lies and subterfuge. By joining the Resistance, they stepped outside the law and away from the mainstream of public opinion.

Despite the battles of May and June, the fighting had left France relatively untouched. It helped to legitimise Vichy. Most people accepted Pétain and his ministers' authority and lived in a grey zone between outright resistance and collaboration. Yet, in that grey zone there were many who could be tempted by a bribe to denounce them to the police. Marion had to be careful about what she said and keep the truth about what she did a secret. She would learn that it was not safe to trust anyone, and that more than anything, she had to be careful what she said. In the dark years that followed, she was constantly looking out for a stranger dawdling on the street outside or listening for a footstep on the stairs. The legacy of those years was Marion's fearful reluctance to talk about the war.

Lyon's dramatic topography and confusing layout made it a natural birthplace for the underground. Two major rivers run through city: the Rhône and the Saône, which are crisscrossed by seventeen bridges. The Swiss border was just eighty-seven miles away, and the Alpine valleys in between were the perfect hideouts.

Although Pierre and Marion wanted to fight the Germans, they had no weapons. The only thing they could do was to counter Vichy propaganda and try to weaken support for the regime through flyers, pamphlets, and eventually, newspapers.

Pierre found a job as a salesman for the Comptoir de la Nawcante, a fishing tackle company. It was the perfect cover to move around the region without drawing attention to himself. While distributing newspapers in the remote villages and towns in the Alps, he began to identify those who sympathised with the cause. Pierre was a keen skier, and it is more than likely he went to Val d'Isère, where Dr. Pétri lived, and was aware of anti-Vichy sympathies in the village where Huguette would eventually be hidden.

It did not take long for the pamphlets and newsletters to come to the attention of the Nazis and the French police. German military intelligence, the Abwehr, had an office in Lyon even though it broke the terms of the armistice. Any individual suspected of spreading anti-German propaganda was put under surveillance. It was not long before informers began to infiltrate the Resistance groups and the police started to arrest Marion and Pierre's friends.

Despite the danger, Pierre turned to sabotage and was soon cutting telephone wires and slashing tires to undermine industrial production—hitting the Germans where it hurt.

Despite the myths that have been spun about the Resistance, it was, for most of the war, dangerously fractured and treacherous. Many of those involved in the Resistance in Lyon had political agendas that set them against one another. Pierre had joined the Resistance to fight for the restitution of the France he believed in, where he had had equal rights with all other French citizens, but he kept the fact that he was Jewish a secret. It was a game Marion's father had already taught her to play. Many *résistants* drawn into the shadowy networks in Lyon had no respect for humanitarian values at all and would double-cross you, especially if you were a Jew.

Henri Frenay was one of the principal Resistance leaders in the Free Zone and the founder of Combat, one of its most important movements. Frenay, and many of those gathered around him, had been members of Action française and he was a vicious anti-Semite. Frenay and his supporters had only joined the Resistance because they opposed Vichy's collaboration with the Nazis, not because they were averse to its politics.

⚜

When Johannes arrived back in Paris, the atmosphere was dystopian. Nazi flags hung along the rue de Rivoli and the streets were teeming with friendly German soldiers, who had orders from Berlin to avoid confrontation. The shops were still full, but the parks were strangely silent, as the birds had disappeared. The black smoke that had settled over the city in June when the large oil and gas tanks had been set on fire during the invasion had killed them all.

Johannes was not the only Jew who returned home in autumn of 1940—over a third of those who had fled went back to the capital as the winter drew in. In retrospect, it seems a strange thing to have done, but the German occupation of France was markedly different from the invasion of Poland in 1939. Synagogues were not burned to the ground but stayed open and became hubs of support for the Jewish community. Many Jews were exactly like the rest of the French; they thought that they could learn to live with the occupation. The Germans hoped to co-opt France as an ally and exploit the country economically. The Wehrmacht soldiers had strict orders not to offend people, as the Nazis did not have the capability to carry out a draconian occupation.

The approach was different, but the fundamental ideology had not changed. On September 5, twenty-seven-year-old Obersturmführer Theodor Dannecker, the new Judenberater, the Adviser on Jewish Affairs, had walked into his office on Avenue Foch. A tall, slender, blond, blue-eyed man, Dannecker was a fanatical anti-Semite, and one of Adolf Eichmann's most trusty lieutenants. It was Eichmann's job to organise and coordinate Hitler's anti-Semitic policies for his boss, the director of the Reich Main Security Office, SS Obergruppenführer Reinhard Heydrich.

Dannecker and Eichmann had already begun experimenting with plans to rid the area controlled by the Nazis of its Jewish population. By the end of January 1940, they had deported 78,000 Jews from the Reich to a "reservation" in Nisko near Lublin in Poland. The plan was based on the US system on Indian reservations, but failed when the terrible conditions were widely reported in the world's press and Hitler abandoned the project. The idea of moving large numbers of Jews by incentive or coercion was not exclusively a Nazi idea. In the late 1930s, the Poles and the French had discussed the resettlement of Jews on the island of Madagascar in the Indian Ocean. Eichmann and Dannecker had spent the summer of 1940 mulling over the logistics of the scheme now that they had control of French ports. It is one of history's strange *What ifs*? If those identified as Jews had been shipped off to Madagascar, would the Holocaust never have happened? Would Johannes, Edith, and their daughters have starved to death on a tropical island or simply been left in peace? The plan fizzled out, however, as France did not hand over control of its navy or its overseas territories, and the failed invasion of Britain had left the British firmly in control of the shipping lanes. A new solution had to be devised, but what that would be even Eichmann had no idea.

By the time Johannes arrived back in Paris, yellow notices all over the city marked out Jewish shops, hairdressers, and restaurants. Until it was forbidden, they were often surrounded by the owner's war medals and citations. Soon, the yellow placards disappeared, only to be replaced by red signs indicating that the premises were now under new Aryan management. Then in late October 1940, Jews were told to register at their local town hall. It was an order Johannes ignored. He had, after all, practised being an invisible Jew for years, but before he disappeared into the shadows, he took an enormous risk.

Under the cover of darkness, Johannes returned to the family apartment on rue Miromesnil to collect anything of value, including Edith's silver coffee set, which now sits on Huguette's sideboard in San Francisco. If Edith had taken it to the south of France, it would have disappeared in the turmoil that was to come. A thief in his own home, Johannes must have taken his shoes off in case the neighbours below heard his footsteps on the creaking parquet floor and crept around in his socks, hoping his wooden foot did not give its telltale tap. He took the silver coffee set he and Edith had been given as a wedding present, not because it meant something to his wife, but because it could, if needed, be sold. He then left as quickly as he could.

With no other way to make money, Johannes became a black marketeer in the shady Parisian underworld. It was a risky place in which you had to negotiate a dangerous path between criminals, collaborators, and resisters. Johannes left no account of what happened during the time he spent in wartime Paris. There are no letters, no diary, and he never spoke to his daughters about it. He would die long before survivors gave detailed testaments, but I think I would have preferred not to talk about loss, failure, and betrayal, and if he was involved in the Resistance, he would have kept it secret, just as Marion did. But in her eyes, he had abandoned her mother and given up the fight.

♣

The Holocaust is far from being just an historical fact for those whose lives are marked by it, as mine has been since I met my husband. It can unexpectedly appear at the most mundane moment, like a ghostly messenger from the past that has traveled through time looking for you.

One summer evening in 2003, Huguette, who was visiting the family in London, came over for dinner with Marion. I was chopping onions in the kitchen when she arrived. She was bubbling with news of a strange discovery. Her family's belongings and all the furniture from 59 rue Miromesnil had been taken to a warehouse near the Gare d'Austerlitz. They were then shipped to Germany, where they were carefully stored in another warehouse, only to be returned to France after the war. The entire contents of the family home were stolen. After the war, the French authorities placed a notice in a newspaper reporting that property had been recovered. Marion had no reason to know the small advertisement was there and missed it.

As a result, everything was auctioned off. It was incomprehensible that chairs and tables could have made the journey eastward and returned intact when 76,000 people did not.

Huguette is convinced that a valuable picture that hung over the fireplace disappeared without a trace. Her discovery was bizarre, but it was sinister as well. This was not a story of neighbours helping themselves, but rather, state requisition of everything the Müllers owned—their sheets, towels, and kitchen utensils, right down to their underwear. It was the first step in an evolving plan to wipe Marion and Huguette's family off the face of the earth and leave no trace of them whatsoever.

The theft was highly organised and named *Aktion Mobel* (Operation Furniture). Its commander, Colonel Kurt von Behr, kept meticulous records and photographic evidence of his work. Although he committed suicide in 1945, in 1948, American soldiers found some of the pictures he had commissioned. They then lay gathering dust in a German archive in Koblenz until 2004, when they were rediscovered. The photographs show baskets full to the brim with lightbulbs and trestle tables laden down with everything from stolen plates to toys. The contents of 38,000 Parisian houses and apartments were taken in hundreds of trains to Germany. As I look at the photos, I wonder if anything belongs to our family.

From 1943 onward, some of the stolen furniture was taken to Lévitan department store on rue du Faubourg Saint-Martin in the 10th arrondissement. The elegantly designed shop had been liquidated in July 1941, as its owner was Jewish. Here items were polished, cleaned, repaired, and put on sale for only the Nazis to browse and buy. The furniture was laid out in showrooms—empty rooms that had lost their owners, one after the other. The shop was staffed by 795 Jewish prisoners from the Drancy internment camp north of Paris, who slept on the fourth floor. After the war, the shop was returned to its owners, but they soon sold it and for many years the building sat empty. It eventually became the headquarters of a PR company, who put on an exhibition about the Nazi shop. My sister-in-law in Paris works in advertising and because she did business with the company, she was invited with her husband to the opening. They were surprised to find it was a cocktail party where champagne was served. The PR company has moved on, but I wonder if at night the ghosts of brooms, pails, pots, and pans come out to haunt the building—and perhaps the ghosts of those who used them.

CHAPTER 6

The Invasion

On June 22, 1941, Hitler invaded the Soviet Union. The French Communist Party, who until this moment had held back from outright resistance because of the Nazi-Soviet Pact, now became an underground force to be reckoned with in industrial Lyon.

The Resistance became increasingly violent, and it was not long before it began to receive support from Churchill's Special Operations Executive, SOE. Pierre began to work with the SOE agents who arrived in the city and finally got the weapons to fight his war. Lyon is surrounded by vast flood plains that were ideal for parachute drops of guns and explosives. Soon Pierre was blowing up factories and railway lines.

On the Riviera, the invasion of the Soviet Union had also placed Edith and Huguette in greater danger than ever before as the extreme right radicalised in the face of the common enemy—communism. In Nice, Joseph Darnand, the head of the Légion française des combattants, formed a paramilitary group, the Service d'ordre légionnaire, known by its initials SOL. It attracted men who were used to the violent life on the rough streets of Nice. Anti-parliamentary and virulently racist, it was a popular movement, and in February 1942, 2,000 members were sworn in during a ceremony that took place in the ruins of the Roman amphitheatre in the hilltop suburb of Cimiez. SOL held torch-lit parades and were regularly seen in their distinctive uniforms marching through the streets of Cannes chanting anti-communist and anti-Semitic slogans. Physical attacks on Jews were rare in France, but in Nice, people reading newspapers on the benches of the seafront Promenade des Anglais were beaten up simply because they looked like Jews.

The summer brought with it a wave of denunciations as people picked up their pens and wrote to local officials and even to Pétain himself. The paper may now be yellowed and the cursive letters in blue ink faded, but passion and hatred still leap off the page. In the National Archives in Paris is a letter sent to Pétain on September 20, 1941, by MD, a resident of Cannes's Avenue de France. MD wrote to tell the Marshal that "we want a French Cannes and not an international town where the Jews are the masters in control and only slaves allowed to live." MD demanded that Jews should be forced to wear a yellow hat, condemned to forced labour and their money confiscated and given to the poor. Ideally, MD thought they should be "made to disappear in bottomless boats to feed the fish they deprive us of."

It was at this perilous moment that Edith decided that Sunday mornings were no longer to be spent in church. She rejected Johannes's ways and, instead, Huguette and her mother went hiking in the hills. It was an assertion of her individual will and identity. Every evening, Huguette remembers that, without fail, she tuned the dial of her radio to listen to the BBC, hoping the neighbours would not hear; if caught, they faced a fine or even imprisonment. The first four notes of Beethoven's Symphony No. 5, *po-po-po-pom*, were followed by the opening words, "*Ici Londres! Les Français parlent aux Français . . .*", "This is London! The French speak to the French . . ." The news came first, and as the summer drew on, it included reports of the mass murder of Jews in the Polish territories previously occupied by the Soviet Union, and then in the Soviet Union itself as the Germans crossed the pre-1939 border. On December 7, the Japanese attacked the American fleet in Pearl Harbor, and on December 11, Hitler declared war on the United States. The same day, he met with his top officials to make clear that he wanted all Jews in the territories controlled by the Nazis to be systematically killed.

In the early hours of Friday, December 12, the French police—accompanied by German soldiers—began ringing the doorbells at some of the smartest addresses in Paris, many of them in and around rue Miromesnil. They arrested 743 French Jews, among them middle-aged doctors, lawyers, and university professors, all of whom were veterans of World War I. Fifty-five of them held the Légion d'Honneur, the country's highest order of merit. The men were taken by train to an internment camp in Compiègne, which was under exclusive German control. It sent out a clear message that no Jew was too important not to be arrested.

Edith and Johannes had no idea that the murderous hands of the Nazis had already claimed the family's first victim. On November 7, 1941, Johannes's younger brother, Rudolph, died of starvation in Gross-Rosen concentration camp. He had been baptised a Lutheran and married a Christian. They lived on a farm south of Dresden. In 1933, he decided that he was of no interest to the Nazis and that he would stay in Germany. The Gestapo caught him hiding in a barn on the family farm, where his family had tried to save him. His children would grow up behind the Iron Curtain and eventually the family lost contact with them.

CHAPTER 7

The Conference

January 1942 was one of the coldest months of the war. The north of France was paralysed in an ice storm. In Cannes, temperatures plummeted. The rented house was built for the heat of summer and impossible to keep warm. There was hardly any coal and constant power cuts. Even lightbulbs were in short supply. Edith and Huguette spent their evenings huddled around a candle while the rest of the house lay in darkness. Besieged by the elements, Edith focused on the mundane chores of daily life that never go away, even in wartime. Huguette's jumpers were by now worn-out and needed darning. As Edith tried to turn a few turnips into a tasty soup, in the southwestern suburbs of Berlin, a fateful meeting was about to convene.

Just before noon on Tuesday, January 20, 1942, a fleet of official black cars drove slowly past the two stone cherubs that stood on either side of the driveway of an Italianate villa. They drew up under the colonnaded portico. Out stepped a series of second-rank Nazi officials, some in uniform, others in dark suits. In the hallway, they were greeted by Adolf Eichmann. He had organised the meeting for his superior, the director of the Reich Main Security Office, SS Obergruppenführer Reinhard Heydrich.

Thick snow covered the lawns that led down to the freezing water of Lake Wannsee. The Villa Marlier was part of a development intended to turn the Wannsee into a northern version of Italy's Lake Garda. In 1940, Heydrich was given use of the villa so it could become an SS and Security Police guest house. Elegant and imposing, the Villa Marlier was the perfect place for him to impress his guests and assert his authority. Edith was no doubt familiar with the house; at one time in the life that had already been stolen from her, she and her mother, Henriette, had entertained J Eichenberg AG clients on a boat they moored on the lake. One of the few family photographs that her sister Wally brought with her to London shows the Wertheims on a day out on the shores of the Wannsee before World War I.

The meeting took place in the dining room around a large mahogany table. On the agenda was a plan to "evacuate," a code word for "deport," all of Europe's Jews to Poland, where they would be killed. The fourteen men seated around the table represented the state and Nazi organisations over which Heydrich needed to assert his authority. Ten of them were university graduates, nine of whom had studied law. One was even a judge. They were Johannes's university contemporaries.

For Marion and Huguette, the most critical person at the table was Martin Luther, a balding forty-seven-year-old former interior decorator with horn-rimmed spectacles. Luther was the undersecretary at the Foreign Ministry responsible for liaising with the SS. From this moment onward, it would be his job to persuade, or pressurize, Germany's satellites and allies to hand over their Jewish populations for deportation.

While Eichmann wrote up the notes of the meeting, in Cannes, on the icy Riviera, Edith tuned in to the BBC on the radio. Singapore had fallen. It was one of the worst disasters in British military history. It seemed that nothing could stop the Nazis and their allies.

On March 5, 1942, Dannecker, the blond, blue-eyed Adviser on Jewish Affairs in the French capital, was summoned for a briefing in Berlin. Heydrich and Eichmann had timetabled the deportation of French Jews to start in 1943, but Dannecker was so fired up with excitement that on his return to Paris he began pushing for the date to be moved forward. Eventually, he was allotted a transportation train. The change in the timetable would have devastating consequences for Marion and Huguette.

♣

In the early morning on March 27, 1942, the 4,000 Jewish prisoners held in the Drancy internment camp north of Paris were ordered into the courtyard in the bright spring sunshine. Dannecker read out the names of 565 men, who were then told to collect their belongings. The French police took them to Bourget-Drancy railway station, where they boarded third-class passenger cars. At five o'clock in the afternoon, the train left for the internment camp at Compiègne. There it spent the night in the sidings as another 547 men, the majority of whom had been arrested in December, were forced on board. After their departure, the men's wives, who rushed to police stations demanding to know where their husbands had been taken, were met with a stony silence.

After the train arrived near the main Auschwitz prison camp, the men were marched along a slippery, muddy road to Birkenau a couple of miles away, where a new camp was under construction. The Vichy government made no protest and, significantly, never made any attempt to find out what had happened to them. Only twenty of the men from *convoi* 1 would survive the war.

PART III

THE CHOICE

CHAPTER 8

Two Boys

In San Francisco, Huguette had asked me not only to find the family of Dr. Pétri, but she also wanted to know why other people had helped her. When she decided to ask Yad Vashem to recognise Dr. Pétri as Righteous Among Nations, I was asked by the committee in charge to produce evidence of the danger Marion and Huguette had been in. Looking for answers, I returned to Paris in January 2020.

In the dark, cavernous crypt of the Mémorial de la Shoah, opposite the eternal flame, are the police files on the Jews who registered their names in Paris and the department of the Seine during the Nazi occupation. Those files disappeared in 1944 and were only found decades later in the archives of the Ministry of Veterans Affairs. The Nazi hunter Serge Klarsfeld believes that they were deliberately hidden to conceal the role that the French police played in the Holocaust—the same police who were supposed to protect young women like Marion and Huguette.

Movies and TV series have left the impression that the Nazis were all-powerful and that it was impossible to refuse their demands, but on the ground in France in 1942, things were far from black and white.

In April 1942, the authoritarian Pierre Laval, a fifty-seven-year-old lawyer and former Socialist, was appointed prime minister. He believed collaborating with the Nazis would give France a role in the new European order. He was happy to use Jews, who were not French nationals, as pawns in this power game.

When Dannecker ordered a mass roundup of all Jews in France, Carl Oberg and Helmut Knochen, the German Security police chiefs, knew that they simply did not have the manpower to carry out mass arrests, and were worried what impact German troops arresting Jews on the streets of Paris would have on public opinion. Their top priority was to keep the country calm and malleable so its economy could be exploited for the German war effort. It was clear that the only way to carry out a mass roundup was with the help of the French police, who were sympathetic to problems that it entailed. Sensing the best way forward was a compromise, Laval sent René Bousquet, Vichy's new head of police, to negotiate with the Germans. His brief was to grab back what French sovereignty over the police that he could with the lives of Jews, which he considered expendable.

Bousquet came to an agreement with Knochen that his men would round up 22,000 foreign Jews (a figure later reduced to 20,000), whose names the police held in the register of Jews that is in the Mémorial de la Shoah. That roundup took place in Paris in July 1942.

At first, I thought that the files in the Mémorial de la Shoah had little relevance to Marion and Huguette's story, but standing in front of those files, I realised that they are vital evidence that foreign Jews were targeted for deportation. and that meant that denaturalisation, the sword of Damocles that hung over their heads, was now a death sentence.

From the Adagio hotel in the 15th arrondissement, I look out over Paris. The sitting-room window of my top-floor apartment is eye to eye with the Eiffel Tower. I look down on rue Nélaton, where the Vélodrome d'Hiver, the Winter Cycling Track, once stood. In the roundup that took place from July 16 to 17, 1942, adults without children were moved to Drancy but families were taken to the stadium, which gave its name to the roundup—*la Rafle du Vél d'Hiver*.

Only one photograph of the street on that fateful day has ever been found. It shows the buses lined up outside the entrance. A lone cyclist passes by. Policemen stand guard.

Johannes was living two streets away on rue Desaix. He cannot have failed to see the stream of Renault buses, ones that usually took people to work, bringing frightened men, women, and children to the stadium . . . or was he too scared to look out the window? For days, some 7,000 people were crammed into the stands in boiling heat, without food, water, or lavatories.

The families were eventually transferred to the internment camps at Pithiviers and Beaune-la-Rolande, near Orléans, where, on Bousquet's orders, the police separated the children from their parents, who were moved to Drancy to await deportation. On July 19, 1942, the first French victims were gassed in Auschwitz-Birkenau and in Pithiviers and Beaune-la-Rolande, leaving 4,000 children alone.

Bousquet's men rounded up 13,000 people, 7,000 short of his target. Something significant had happened. Many of the Jews' neighbours made spur-of-the-moment decisions to help them and some policemen tipped them off so they could hide. People were suddenly aware of the danger that the Jews were in. Many of the younger Jews who managed to escape joined the Resistance. Both of these developments would play a crucial role in Marion and Huguette's story.

The street in front of the Vélodrome d'Hiver—known as the "Vél d'Hiv"—
in Paris, on July 16, 1942, during the roundup of the city's Jews.

Not long after I get home, I decide to get rid of an old ugly TV, which was once Marion's, that sits on the shelf in my office. It has been balanced for over ten years on a small leather suitcase that was also hers. I click the catches open. Inside are pictures of the kids on holiday. Postcards they sent her and their drawings and scribbles. In the middle of the pile is a tightly sealed freezer bag containing two newspaper cuttings. One, on which she has written in blue pen "Le Monde, 18 juillet 90," is a report of a memorial service at the site of the former Vél d'Hiv stadium. The other appears to be a list of memorial notices that I can only assume were published at the back the newspaper. It reads:

16–17 JULY 1942
Roundup by the French Vichy police of 4,115 children, among them our brothers:

MAURICE TSETVERY
(9 YEARS)

PAUL SZWARC
(11 YEARS)

Of the 5,919 women, our mothers:

ADÈLE SKORKA-TSETVERY
(39 YEARS)

RUCHLA DUKAT-SZWARC
(37 YEARS)

Of the 3,118 men, our fathers:

NATHAN TSETVERY
(43 YEARS)

LEJBUS SZWARC
(45 YEARS)

At the bottom it says, "two sons escaped, former resistants and fighting Jews." For the first time since she died, I feel that Marion is in the room trying to tell me something. It was as if she had left yet another clue, that one day she hoped someone would find.

Clicking around on the Internet, I find pictures of two of the boys on the Mémorial de la Shoah website.

Maurice is a rather sad, serious, old-fashioned-looking child with dark eyes. In contrast, Paul was photographed with his brother Joseph. If the picture was in colour, it would look completely modern. Paul wears a turtleneck sweater and his brother, a bomber jacket.

The pictures were given to the memorial by their brothers Joseph Szwarc and Leon Tsetvery. No one in our family has ever heard of these men. The latter had an elder brother, Jacques, who was a little bit younger than Marion. They had all escaped the roundup and

Paul Szwarc, left, with his brother Joseph Szwarc, right; and Maurice Tsetvery, in undated photos taken before they were rounded up in July 1942.

joined the Resistance, which I am left to conclude is where Marion must have met them.

On August 13, it was decided that the children would be deported with adult Jews, who would be moved to Drancy from the Free Zone. The optimum ratio was set as 300 adults to 500 children. This decision was made not to alleviate the children's suffering, but to trick the railway workers so they would assume they were families. When the children arrived at Drancy, they were ill, their clothes filthy and torn. At night they were locked in alone, 120 to a room.

When the deportations began, the children were woken at five o'clock in the morning. It was still dark, and it was impossible to get them to come down to the courtyard. French policemen had to go up into the rooms and carry them down as they struggled and screamed. Among them were Paul Szwarc, who was taken on *convoi* 22 that left for Auschwitz on August 21. Maurice Tsetvery was deported on *convoi* 23 on August 24. Two little boys, who died with strangers, whose story Marion felt was important enough to have it kept among the kids' drawings and scribbles and photos of their happy smiling faces. Their brothers must have played an important role in her life.

The deportations radicalised the Jews who had survived, like Leon Tsetvery and Joseph and Jacques Szwarc. They realised that it was not enough to simply join the Resistance, but that an exclusive Jewish resistance was needed. Marion was drawn into their world when a few months later in December 1942, she found herself alone and in danger.

♣

Bousquet's second roundup happened right on Edith and Huguette's doorstep. Edith would have heard the rumours that were rife along the Riviera. Desperate, many Jews committed suicide.

Then something happened that goes a long way toward answering Huguette's question—"Why did people help me?" On August 23, seventy-two-year-old Archbishop Jules-Géraud Saliège decided to take a stand against the Vichy government. After he was told about the deportations from Drancy by a Jewish communist, Saliège made a radical move, issuing a statement that read: "Jews are real men and women. Foreigners are real men and women. . . . They are part of the human species. They are our brothers, like anyone else. A Christian cannot forget that." His words were published in underground newspapers and broadcast back to France on the BBC. He was supported by other senior bishops, and during their sermons, priests across the Free Zone read his statement from their pulpits. It reminded many of those in the grey zone of indifference—those who were not driven by the passions of resistance and collaboration—where their moral compass should lie.

Saliège, however, could do nothing to stop the roundup. Three days later, at five o'clock in the morning, French police began knocking on the doors of Jewish homes and hotel rooms along the Côte d'Azur. Edith must have sat at home fearful of a knock on the door.

Then something else surprising happened. Although there were plenty of anti-Semites in France, large numbers of people saw the roundup of the Jews for what it was—French collaboration with the Nazis. In Cannes, "Free the Jews" was scrawled on walls and benches on the seafront and near the town hall. Leaflets against the arrests and the deportations were distributed in Nice and in several other spots along the Côte d'Azur.

Laval quickly realised the danger he was in. In a broadcast on June 22, he had already shocked the nation when he said he "wished for a German victory," because otherwise, "Bolshevism [would] establish itself everywhere." To save his political skin, he told the Nazis he would not hand over any more Jews. Although Eichmann had scheduled forty-five convoys of a thousand Jews each, not one single convoy left France for Auschwitz between September 15 and October 31. Knochen understood Laval's dilemma and there were no reprisals. Bousquet could have refused his orders in July, but he dared not try. The government in Vichy did not take any reprisals against Saliège, either.

CHAPTER 9

The Identity Card

Six months after Marion died in 2010, clearing out her wardrobe, I stumbled across a small, battered, dark-blue booklet the size of a credit card holder. Inside, stuck to the covers, was an official document with a picture of Marion in her early twenties in the right-hand corner. It was a *carte d'identité*, her French identity card. The photograph was unmistakably of Marion, but there was something odd about it. She had long hair and her expression was unusually demure. Marion always had a broad, bright smile in photographs. To my complete surprise, I quickly noticed these were not the papers of Marion Müller, but of someone named Juliette Giraud, who had been born Juliette Détraz in March 1919 in a place called Chevenoz that I had never heard of. At the bottom, Marion had written in pencil *Ellen Marion Müller*. It was a message from beyond the grave.

Marion was always perfectly French in her tastes and manners. Now I understood why. She had had to be in order to impersonate a young woman born in France. She had her father to thank for that. Before the war, she had dreamed of becoming an actress. Now she had to play a role that had to be convincing, or she could lose her life. Blending in to avoid arrest was a form of resistance, and that made Marion an agent in her own survival. It turned her into a fiercely independent and self-reliant person.

Jews in France were never confined to ghettos, nor were they forced underground like Anne Frank. They lived in the open and this required a unique set of survival tactics. Marion may have disliked her father, but the little blue booklet shows she was more like him than she cared to admit.

The Vichy government had made it compulsory for everyone over the age of sixteen to carry a *carte d'identité*, and from 1942 onward all Jews were supposed to have the word *Juif*—Jew—stamped on their card in red. Some people thought it wise to obey the law, but others were more wary and chose to lie about who they were. Some French may have begun to show the Jews sympathy after the roundups in the summer of 1942 and tried to help, but there were still plenty of people who were willing to inform on them. The false identity card was a stark reminder of the danger Marion was in.

The card was issued in Lyon in April 1943. Vichy had just introduced new rules, which meant ID cards now had to show the number under which the person was registered. Marion's was 9064. The card says she was married. So, Marion and Pierre must have pretended that they were legally a couple. It gives Marion's address as 30 Montée du Gourgillon, a steep cobbled street that winds up the hill from the heart of medieval Lyon. In the 1940s, it was an unsanitary and rundown working-class district, but, more importantly, it was the perfect resistance address. The houses are built into the hillside with narrow passageways, or *traboules*, running between them. It is possible to enter on the ground floor of one building and leave it by the higher floor of another. From the top of the street, there is a panoramic view across the city. It was perfect for watching out for approaching police vans.

Marion's *carte d'identité*, issued in April 1943.

By the summer of 1942, Marion's life had become increasingly risky. Since the British had lent the Resistance support, the movement had grown exponentially. There were frequent parachute drops, and sabotage attacks became more and more violent. In face of the growing threat, Bousquet's police stepped up their hunt to break the underground networks, and in September, Laval authorised the deployment of several hundred Gestapo agents in the Free Zone. The dangers of betrayal and infiltration mounted as the Gestapo launched a series of brutal raids.

In November 1942, after the Allied landings in North Africa, the Germans occupied the Free Zone. Train after train of German troops arrived in Lyon. Tanks and trucks were not far behind. The clocks were set to German time, swastikas were raised on public buildings, and the Gestapo's black Citroëns were seen all over the city. Lyon was to pay the price for its defiance. Klaus Barbie, a sadistic twenty-nine-year-old SS officer, became the Gestapo chief. He personally tortured and executed many of his prisoners. The entire resistance operation was soon riddled with infiltrators, and Britain's SOE secret agents fled the city. It was not long before Pierre was picked up by Barbie's men.

One Sunday lunch when my husband was away, my children started asking questions about the resistance in Lyon. He was very protective of his mother, so they knew it was better to be pushy when he was not there. Marion told them that in autumn of 1942, Pierre had been taken in for questioning but before he was tortured, he had managed to escape from the cellars. She said he was helped by a French woman who worked in the building as a maid. It was a confusing story. More than anything, I could not understand what a maid was doing in a Nazi prison.

Ten years later, as I drove around Lyon and visited the city's two notorious former prisons, it slowly dawned on me that the place Pierre had been taken was the Hôtel Terminus, Barbie's HQ. Today, the hotel is the Mercure Lyon Centre Château Perrache. Not realising it was once the Terminus, I had briefly thought about reserving a room. When I scrolled down through the reviews, I saw that plenty of guests complained about the hard beds and the bad plumbing, but no one had mentioned that the story of what happened there during World War II had kept them awake at night. It is hidden away under a splash of garish primary colours. On the third floor, Barbie plunged prisoners into scalding and then freezing water and hung them upside down. In his 1988 documentary, *The Life and Times of Klaus Barbie,* Marcel Ophuls interviewed Barbie's victims, who described how in the flick of a switch he turned from a calm interrogator into a raving sadist.

After his escape from the Terminus, Pierre knew his life was in danger. He had to leave Lyon as soon as possible and decided to try to join General de Gaulle's Free French Forces in London. On Christmas Day 1942, Pierre set out across the Pyrenees. SOE agent Hugh Dormer, who was later killed in action, described the journey. It was, he said, an ordeal he had been entirely unprepared for. "As we finally came opposite and underneath the actual peak which we were to cross, the sight filled me with awe and dread," he recalled. The vineyards were terraced, and Dormer found himself slipping on loose rubble and stones even on the lower slopes. Then came steep climbs and vertiginous descents alongside frozen lakes. It was midwinter, and Pierre, like hundreds of others, would wade through the snow in his ordinary clothes. Marion refused to go with him, convinced that she would not survive the journey.

On a trip in 2007 with Marion to the Pyrenees Grande Cascade de Gavarnie, France's highest waterfall, I took the chance of asking her if she was really convinced that she would have lost her footing and plunged into a ravine. She was an extremely fit women who loved skiing and was used to the mountains. Marion flicked her hand across her face and laughed, "I could never do that! Look at it!" She pointed at the waterfall, which was admittedly crashing down a sheer cliff face. Her pace then speeded up as she edged in front of me. I was left with the feeling that, as ever, she was not telling the whole story. I wonder now if she was frightened of leaving her mother and Huguette alone. I think she hoped that she could protect them both. Her failure to do so was something she could never come to terms with.

All those who went to join de Gaulle's Free French became outlaws. They were stripped of their French citizenship and condemned as criminals. It required a rare courage and resolution to take such a step, but in doing so, Pierre abandoned Marion in one of the most dangerous places in France. Barbie was determined to hunt down every Jew he could get his hands on. Now in intense danger, she had to find a way to survive on her own. Without Pierre she would be drawn into an exclusively Jewish resistance movement that was not just fighting to end the occupation, but against annihilation. The ID card was about to reveal a story of how Jews saved Jews in a DIY humanitarian rescue mission. This is where the brothers of the two little boys, Maurice Tsetvery and Paul Szwarc, must have come into Marion's life. In the months that followed, they must have been among her closest friends. From members of the Jewish resistance, like the Szwarc and Tsetvery brothers, Marion would have learned the details of the roundup in Paris. It must have left her with few illusions of what would happen if you were caught.

In the summer of 1942, as Bousquet began his manhunt, the youth section of the Union générale des israélites de France, an organisation that had been set up by Vichy at the insistence of the Nazis, went underground. The youth movement was one of the UGIF's six departments, the Sixième and the resistance movement they formed was known as the Sixième, the Sixth. In May, the leaders of the Sixième met secretly in the university town of Montpellier with the Mouvement de jeunesse sioniste, the Young Zionist Movement. They had also gone underground and formed a resistance movement. From now on the two groups would work in tandem, forging identity papers and documents. They also hid Jewish children and took many of them secretly across the border into Spain or Switzerland. Additionally, they created an armed partisan movement, the Armée juive, which was a proper militia of almost 2,000 armed men and women. Oddly, in most of the Holocaust and resistance museums in France, there is no mention of the Armée juive. In the crypt of the Mémorial de la Shoah, it is the fighters of the Warsaw ghetto who are remembered—not France's own Jewish partisans. Yet, it was this network that offered Marion a lifeline and saved the lives of thousands of others. Joseph Szwarc's older brother, Jacques, who was just a few years younger than Marion, was a Sixième courier and forger.

Etan Guinat, a chemist, and his wife Lili were Jewish refugees from Germany. In 1942, they were key members of the Young Zionist Movement. In Lyon and Grenoble, they also made false papers and took children across the border to Switzerland. The couple gave a video testament that I listen to on the website of the United States Holocaust Memorial Museum. Etan's testimony concentrates on his military activities, and it is only when Lili Guinat begins to talk that I understand the importance of Marion's false ID card and her relationship with the Szwarc brothers. Obtaining a new identity was far more complicated than writing any old name at random and stamping the card with what looked like an official stamp. It was crucial that the person's name on the papers was registered in a local municipality. The blue ID card was just one of a whole ream of papers in the name of Juliette Girard that Marion would have been given, among them birth and marriage certificates and—crucially—ration cards.

Lili Guinat was three years younger than Marion. In the video, she is smartly dressed and her hair is immaculate. Her outfit is topped off with a statement necklace. She reminds me of Marion. Lili describes in detail how it was a woman's job to go to small towns and villages in the Alps in the departments of Isère, Haute-Savoie, and Savoie to contact officials who might help. In this way the Jewish resistance developed a crucial network of people who could offer help and protection. After the 1942 roundups, some local officials in the Alps decided that it was their duty to do something to help the Jews. Lili was the first of the female couriers to establish contact with them. As I listen to her, I wonder if she and Marion may have known each other.

Lili explains that when the women arrived in a village their first point of contact was the local priest, whom they would ask if the local mayor was sympathetic to their plight. If he was, he would organise for duplicate ID and ration cards to be issued in the name of people who were already registered in the municipality. If somebody was stopped by the police and their identity had to be verified, the police would ring the town hall and ask for confirmation that the person was indeed registered with them. This way the Jewish resistance established a network in the French Alps. Female resistance workers would travel to the towns and villages to collect the ration cards that were issued on a monthly basis. It is not clear from Lili's testament if the person whose ID was cloned was informed.

When young women were given false identities, if they spoke good French and could pass as French, they were recruited to support this fast-growing network. Marion must have been among them, as she would have known from Pierre's resistance activities who was likely to be a sympathiser. It is more than likely that is why she went regularly to Val d'Isère. This was why she must have trusted Dr. Pétri when he offered to hide Huguette. She never mentioned this to Huguette out of fear she might break her cover by saying something to another young person who might report it back to their parents.

The Jewish resistance also collected deliveries of cash from Switzerland that came from the American Joint Jewish Distribution

Committee to support their activities. Etan Guinat says that it was the girls who picked up the money. This is the missing background to a story Marion told, after we had hired a boat on Lake Annecy during the school holidays. Marion laughed as the children related the adventure over lunch, adding that she had once been on a boat on the lake with a suitcase of money that had fallen into the water. She had to dry the notes on the grassy shore in the sunshine, she told them. When I asked what she was doing with a suitcase of money, she waved her hand and said, "moving it around," and then started clearing the table.

Listening to Lili Guinat, it becomes clear to me that Juliette Détraz was a real person. When I type her name into Google, the documents that come up confirm that her parents were, as the ID card says, Eloi Joseph Détraz and Berthe Franceline Sache. Chevenoz is a small mountain village above Lake Geneva.

When I look up Chevenoz on the map, I am stunned to find out that in the summer of 2006 we spent a week with Marion on a family holiday in the village of Le Biot, just south of Chevenoz. She never said a word. Maybe it had completely slipped her mind, but I doubt it. She would have had to learn the names of the streets, the mayor, the priest, the doctor, the butcher, and the baker. In 2006, Détraz was still alive. She lived in the little village of Saint-Jean-d'Aulps, next to Le Biot. Marion and I went to the supermarket in the village more than once. Perhaps we walked past Détraz with our shopping trolley. I wonder if she ever knew her identity had been cloned. On Marion's side, I suppose old habits die hard. Once you have had it drummed into you that you must not talk about who you are, you assume that is the norm.

Juliette Détraz and her parents are buried in nearby Thonon-les-Bains close to the Swiss border. When we ask at the cemetery office in Thonon-les-Bains if they can locate the grave, the woman behind the desk asks anxiously if we are members of the family. She is hoping someone has come to pay the cemetery dues. Juliette Détraz is buried with her parents and her husband, Bernard Hel. There is no trace online of her having ever married a man named Giraud. The grave will take its secrets with it as it is due to be destroyed at the end of the year and the family's bones moved to an ossuary.

Thonon-les-Bains was home of a significant resistance movement. The Secrétaire du Commissariat de police in Thonon, Paul Gruffat, was born in Chevenoz and has been recognised as Righteous Among Nations. It was here that President Chirac inaugurated a monument to the Righteous in 1997. I send an email to the town hall in Chevenoz, but to my surprise they reply that there was no resistance movement in the village. They do tell me that in 1943, the mayor was Michel Mercier. His sense of duty helped to save Marion from the Nazis, but his activities seem to have been so secret that they have been completely forgotten.

It took considerable bravery to work as a courier, and the Jewish underground saved thousands of Jewish lives. The title Righteous Among Nations is only awarded to non-Jews who saved Jews. It is one reason that its heroes are forgotten. One of them was Marion.

CHAPTER 10

The Reprieve

In early November 1942, rumours that the Italians were about to occupy Nice began to circulate along the Riviera. Until Italy was unified in 1860, Nice had been part of the Kingdom of Piedmont-Sardinia. It was also the birthplace of Giuseppe Garibaldi, the Italian nationalist leader, who was a key player in the unification of Italy. In return for French support for unification, Nice and its surroundings and the parts of the Duchy of Savoy in the Alps were immediately ceded to France in a rigged plebiscite. The Italian fascist leader Mussolini had invaded France in 1940 in the hope that he could seize the territory back. Edith grabbed the opportunity and immediately packed her suitcase. She and Huguette caught the train to Nice. If Nice was occupied by the Italians, it would be far safer than Cannes. Although the Racial Laws that had been introduced in Italy in 1938 were far harsher than the Nuremberg Laws, there had as yet been no deportations from Italy.

As Edith fled, the Nazis claimed their second victim in the family. Johannes's mother, Ida, committed suicide in Scheveningen, a suburb of The Hague, today just north of the International Criminal

Court. She poisoned herself with cyanide. In Holland, the round-ups that had also begun in July were far more violent than those in France. An elderly widow, she could not face the horror of being caught. Johannes's father had died in 1938. Petrified, Ida found herself all alone in a foreign country. She is a forgotten victim of the Nazis. Her name does not appear on any memorials or lists. The only thing we know about her is that her father ran a large tanning factory in the now-Polish city of Rybnik, where he is remembered as a generous philanthropist who built schools and orphanages. She is now just a shadowy figure in this story.

Edith rented a small, terraced house on Avenue de Béarn, a quiet street in the hilltop suburb of Cimiez, a fifteen-minute walk from the narrow streets of the old town. Huguette started at a new school that was simply called the Lycée de jeunes filles, the Girls' School.

Huguette has always been shy and retiring. She does not remember the names of any of the girls in her class or year. One of them, however, Simone Jacob, would grow up to be the school's most famous pupil. As Simone Veil, she became a lawyer and campaigner for women's rights, and as Minister for Health, legalized abortion in France. Veil, who was the daughter of an impoverished architect and the youngest of four children, remembered the school as a liberal place where the staff were sympathetic toward their Jewish pupils. Veil's class photo from 1941–42 is on her Wikipedia page. It was taken in the spring before Huguette arrived at the school. The girls are arranged in three rows. As I look at it, I wonder which ones made friends with Huguette and which she disliked.

Edith must have held her breath until at three o'clock on the afternoon of November 11, Italian soldiers in plumed hats were spotted bicycling along the Corniche. Italian army trucks appeared on the coast road. Before long they were seen on the seafront, the Promenade des Anglais. Able to make her own decisions for once,

Simone Veil's 1941–42 class photo from the Lycée de jeunes filles in Nice. She is in the back row, first on the left.

Edith had made the right one. The Italians did not just seize Nice, but took control of the entire southeastern corner of France in a line that ran from Toulon through Gap, Grenoble, Chambéry, and then on to Annecy and the Swiss border, where Marion was spending most of her time.

Within days, an office adjacent to the synagogue at 24 Boulevard Dubouchage was permitted to officially help Jewish refugees in the city. An Italian soldier was even posted at the synagogue to ward off anti-Semitic gangs. The Italians' attitude to the Jews during their occupation of the area was driven first and foremost by the desire to make it as separate from France as possible. The fascist government in Rome was also keen to assert its independence from Germany. At Stalingrad, the Wehrmacht were struggling to hold off the Soviet counteroffensive. The Italians were playing a game that René Bousquet knew well. Once again, the Jews were the pawns in a power game.

The story of the Italian occupation is more often than not confined to the Jewish experience and told in a positive light. While for nine months for the Jews the threat of arrest and deportation disappeared, life became extremely hard. The occupation bred a bitterness and resentment that changed public opinion, fueled resistance, and polarised society. The underground press mushroomed. A bomb explosion at Cannes railway station, on December 18, was followed by numerous attacks on the railways, especially those that fed into the Italian system.

As in the rest of France, which was now under Nazi control, Vichy still had a voice in how Italian-occupied France was run. The French civil service and the police remained in their posts. The violence in the Italian zone boosted Laval's determination to stamp out resistance. At the end of February, at the Municipal Casino in Nice, in front of giant portraits of Pétain and Laval, a huge crowd gathered to watch the inauguration of the militia, the Milice française, considered by the Resistance to be even more dangerous than the Gestapo. By 1944, the Milice had at least 30,000 members. They spoke local dialects and had extensive knowledge of the towns and countryside.

Mussolini's secret police, the Organizzazione per la Vigilanza e la Repressione dell'Antifascismo, or OVRA, were also quick to respond to the growing resistance. They were just as vicious as the Gestapo. From their headquarters in Nice, even though they left Jews alone, they set out to hunt down *résistants*, communists, and freemasons. Italian military units carried out operations against resistance networks across the occupied sector and were supported by Blackshirts, Mussolini's militia. In Cimiez, prisoners were interrogated and tortured in the Villa Lynwood, which was known as the "Villa of Torture." After the OVRA had finished with them, the prisoners were moved to internment camps in nearby Sospel, Embrun, or Modane, or to jails in Italy.

Local anger and resentment were also fueled by food shortages that got worse and worse as the occupation went on. The situation across France was dire, but after the liberation of North Africa, trade routes across the Mediterranean were cut. Salted fish, vegetables, wine, and eggs simply disappeared from the shelves. By the spring of 1943, a famine was a real possibility. Many people left Nice for the countryside and there were frequent demonstrations in front of the city's town hall. On Bastille Day, on July 14, at a demonstration in Place Masséna, Gaullists unfurled the Tricolour and sang "La Marseillaise."

Most people in Nice read *L'Eclaireur*, a right-wing newspaper, which, because of a shortage of paper, was now a two-page newsletter dominated by small ads and cinema listings. I am sure Edith read the paper on the benches on the Promenade des Anglais. The newspaper was one way to keep track of the latest ration quotas that changed every month and were front-page news. The other headlines were a pack of lies. In January 1943, *L'Eclaireur* claimed that the Germans were winning the battle of Stalingrad.

At the end of the month, however, the gossip on the Promenade des Anglais took an alarming turn when a violent roundup took place in Marseille. The city was full of Jewish refugees, but since the fall of North Africa had made an invasion of Europe's Mediterranean a possibility, the last thing the Nazis wanted was vital ports like Marseille brimming with what they regarded as a dangerous fifth column living in the old run-down streets along the portside. On Bousquet's orders, 12,000 French police were brought into the city to help the Germans carry out a major operation against the Jews.

The roundup began around the opera house on the evening of Friday, January 22. At dusk the following day, buses began moving through the gloomy streets toward the portside slums of Le Panier, the oldest part of the city. The police ordered everyone out of their homes, telling them to bring with them the barest minimum for an overnight stay. They were given the impression that they would be away for a matter of hours. When the thousands of residents who had been arrested were finally released, they returned to find that their homes had been dynamited. They received no help from the town hall and no compensation. The operation was the pinnacle of Franco-German cooperation during the war and an event that oddly few people outside of Marseille remember.

Type the name "René Bousquet" into Google, and one of the first things that comes up is a black-and-white photograph of him taken

At the Hôtel de Ville in Marseille, January 23, 1943, front row, left to right: SS Sturmbannführer Bernhard Griese; Vichy prefect Antoine Lemoine; Rolf Mühler, commander of Marseilles' Sicherheitspolizei (military police); and René Bousquet, secretary general of the Vichy French police.

in the town hall in Marseille on the second day of the operation. He is wearing a fur-trimmed winter coat and has a broad smile on his face. In his right hand, a cigarette dangles from his fingers. Alongside Bousquet are the city's *préfet*, Pierre Barraud, and the Nazi commanders who came from Paris to oversee the operation. One of them is laughing. Bousquet's men had captured women with small children, old women in black shawls bent by age, and frightened teenagers. They had loaded them all directly onto freight cars. Not long after the roundup, Heinrich Himmler, one of the key architects of the "Final Solution," traveled to Paris to congratulate Bousquet—but the smile was about to be wiped off his face. Within weeks, the Nazis informed the police chief that almost six hundred French citizens were in Drancy awaiting deportation. They asked for his permission to transfer them to the east.

For Bousquet, it was a dangerous moment. Yet again, he had to make a choice. The course of war had now made him more cautious. The Germans had just suffered a major defeat at Stalingrad, and in North Africa, the British had pushed the Wehrmacht across the border into Tunisia. The new European order that Laval had gambled on no longer looked so invincible. The pressure from Berlin to sanction the deportation of the French Jews in Drancy was enormous, but Pétain was adamant that no more French Jews would be allowed to join the "resettlement" convoys. Bousquet was desperate to sustain his working relationship with the Nazi leadership in Paris, but he could not defy Pétain. He tried to curry favour with the Marshal by telling the Germans that the French police would no longer be involved in the deportation process, but gave the green light to the deportation of the six hundred French citizens in Drancy. Most of them were sent to the Sobibor extermination camp in eastern Poland, where there were no selections for slave labour and everyone was gassed. From now on, German police from Saarbrucken were brought in to escort the convoys.

Laval then instructed Bousquet to put forward a new proposal—that all foreign-born Jews who had been granted French citizenship would be immediately denaturalised. It was a move that would free up thousands of people whom he could then allow the Nazis to deport. Johannes, Edith, Marion, and Huguette were now among those Laval and Bousquet considered expendable.

PART IV
A CHINK OF LIGHT

CHAPTER 11

The Photographs

On a hot sunny day, in July 2020, I persuaded my husband to open an old, battered shoebox he had found in his mother's wardrobe. Inside were photographs of Marion when she was young. After she had died, he had been too busy to look at them and put them in a drawer. As the sun streamed in through the window, he picked out a large black-and-white photograph of Marion with a friend and placed it on the bed. The girls were posing on a seafront wall in matching crop tops, pleated miniskirts, and white wedge sandals. To our complete surprise, written in Italian on the sign above their heads was "Comando Presidio Militare Italiano Theoule." Théoule-sur-Mer is just west of Cannes. The picture could only have been taken in the summer of 1943.

At first it seemed that the girls' broad smiles told the story. Under Vichy regulations, they could never have worn these outfits, but the picture was also a tiny act of resistance. After the occupation, the Italian army, fearful of an Allied invasion from North Africa, had begun to reinforce their defences along the coast. By

Left to right: Marion's friend Irène, Huguette, and Marion, at the resort village of Théoule-sur-Mer in 1943.

the time this picture was taken, the Château de Nice had become a vast artillery emplacement. The atmosphere was tense, and in July, Field Marshal Gerd von Rundstedt, the commander-in-chief of Germany's forces on the Western Front, arrived to inspect the defences

Left to right: The first three figures on the left are unknown, Edith (centre), Marion, her friend Irène, and Huguette, in Théoule-sur Mer, 1943.

along the Riviera. Photographs like the one laid out on our bed were completely forbidden.

It was the first in a series of photographs of Marion and her friend with Huguette. In one they were on the deck of a yacht. They are beautiful, tender pictures, but the final photograph was a thunderbolt. The girls were standing by a low wall next to Edith.

They look so happy and relaxed, it was difficult to believe that the pictures were taken in the middle of a war. Edith is dressed in slacks and a shirt. Her hair scooped up neatly in a bun. She looks straight at the camera and has the same radiant smile as Marion. With them is a middle-aged couple and another girl. As I looked at Edith, I wondered who took the picture. Was there an eighth person on this day trip whom she was smiling at?

I wonder if Edith was really as relaxed as she looks in the photograph. I doubt it. Marianne Naquet, a twenty-three-year-old from

Bordeaux, wrote a series of letters to her friend Margarite from the Riviera in the summer of 1943. They were discovered by Margarite's daughter, who published them in a small book, *Lettres de Marianne: lettres d'une jeune fille juive sous l'occupation, décembre 1941–septembre 1943*. Like Huguette, she had gone to Nice with her parents in 1942. The letters say very little as they had to pass the censor, but are full of a sense of foreboding, as Marianne alludes to arrests and deportations. She told her friend that she found her life stifling and even when she spent the afternoon swimming in the sea under a clear blue sky, she felt as if she was suffocating.

How the pictures ended up in the back of my mother-in-law's wardrobe is a story no one can tell us, as Huguette cannot remember anything about that day. The horror of what was about to happen has blanked it out of her mind. My sister-in-law identifies Marion's friend as a young woman named Irène, who she knows nothing about besides the fact that she was killed in a car crash after the war.

There are, however, lots of pictures online of Théoule in the 1930s. It does not take long to identify the beach as the Plage de l'Aiguille, a small cove on the Esterel coast. The next time we are in Cannes we decide to see the beach for ourselves. My husband is determined to find the exact spot where the picture was taken. It does not take him long. The wall has been rebuilt as the town was virtually destroyed during the Allied landings in 1944. He wants to take a new photograph, but I am too frightened to be in it. I think the place is jinxed. As we drive away, I immediately regret refusing to be in the picture. The snapshot was a little act of assertion—proof that evil does not always win.

⚜

In July 1943, Pierre finally arrived in London. As he was eventually parachuted back into France, I had assumed that he was recruited by the SOE. The organisation kept files on all their agents, which are now held in the National Archives not far from Kew Gardens in West London. It is a stone's throw from our home on the other side of the Thames. The files were only declassified in 2015. Pierre's file is stamped SECRET in red ink at both the top and the bottom. Inside there is a small handful of faded papers held together by string that reveal a story I am not expecting.

After Pierre crossed the Pyrenees, although Spain was technically a neutral country, he was arrested. The watches he had brought to sell were most probably confiscated as he then spent six months in a Spanish concentration camp. The camp in Miranda was near a small railway junction at the foot of the Pyrenees. The conditions there were appalling. Prisoners slept on the floor under thin blankets and there was hardly anything to eat. I email the Spanish archive where the camp records are held to see if they have any information. They reply that there is no record of a Pierre Haymann. It is likely he used an alias, but I have no idea what it could have been. The trail goes cold. The British Military Attaché from the embassy in Madrid visited Miranda once a fortnight. It is likely that on one of these visits he negotiated Pierre's release. The papers in Pierre's file say that he was put on a Royal Air Force flight from Gibraltar to RAF Abbotsinch, now Glasgow Airport. It is an indication of just how important Pierre was in the resistance movement in Lyon.

Early in the morning of July 1, 1943, Pierre finally stepped down onto British soil. He was given a hearty breakfast and a cup of sweet, milky tea. It was his first taste of Britain. It must have felt both exhilarating and alien. He could not speak a word of English. It had been almost eight months since he left Marion in Lyon, during which time she had had no word from him. At last, his dream of parachuting back into France to carry on the fight against the Nazis must have felt tantalisingly close. On the Eastern Front, the

Soviets were on the offensive and the biggest tank battle in history, the Battle of Kursk, had just begun. It was a turning point in the war. At last, victory seemed a credible dream.

Pierre was driven to Glasgow Central Station and put on a train for London. As he looked out the window at the green fields, he must have hoped that within weeks he would be reunited with Marion. Yet, when the train pulled into London's Euston Station, British officials were waiting for him on the platform. Pierre was then driven south across the Thames to a leafy, residential street in Wandsworth. He stepped out in front of a vast gothic palace with an array of romantic towers. It was surrounded by barbed wire and patrolled by sentries. Like every other person who had arrived in Britain from occupied Europe since January 1941—even Rudolf Hess, a leading Nazi politician who flew solo to Scotland in the hope of negotiating a peace settlement—Pierre would spend weeks being debriefed in MI5's London Reception Centre in the requisitioned Royal Patriotic School.

New arrivals were told to empty their pockets and hand over their suitcase. They were then shown to a bunk in the dormitory. There they sat and waited, sometimes for days, until they were taken in turn into a large room to be interviewed. A couple of chairs were drawn up at a long, bare table. Pierre's possessions were spread out on the tabletop. They had already been examined by a team of inspectors. Using powerful magnifying glasses, the team had peered at letters, money, pocketbooks, even his keys. Everyday objects like this offered a crucial insight into daily life in war-torn continental Europe. They also could give vital clues that people were not who they claimed they were. If Pierre had any belongings left, after months in the Spanish internment camp, it cannot have added up to much. Maybe he had a picture of Marion that now lay next to his keys and his false ID on the bare table.

The chief interrogator, Oreste Pinto, was known as the "human bloodhound." A multilingual Dutch Jew, he collected wild animals that he later donated to London Zoo. He interviewed 30,000 people during World War II. His technique was to cause an emotional crisis early on in an interrogation, and his tactics were vicious. Pierre was questioned about every detail of his life. His replies were taken down in shorthand by a secretary and typed up into the document that I now hold in my hand. Pierre told the interrogators that his mother had died in 1935. He said that his father lived at 15 rue Cognacq-Jay in Paris not far from the Eiffel Tower. He had a sister and three brothers. A few days later, he was called back. He was asked if he was willing to return to France as a secret agent. Before he responded, to check his commitment and ability to resist interrogation, a dark picture of his future life in the underground was spelt out. The emphasis was on the risks, possible arrest, torture, and execution.

While I was waiting for Pierre's file at the National Archives, I had begun to click about on my computer. I typed in his father's name, Albert Haymann. A picture of Albert immediately popped up on the Mémorial de la Shoah website. He was a tall, well-built man with dark, soft eyes and a bushy moustache. In the photograph, he was dressed in a smart suit and tie.

While Pierre was at the Patriotic School, there was a knock at the door of his apartment at 15 rue Cognacq-Jay. The police had come to arrest sixty-seven-year-old Albert. His family had lived in France for generations. Laval may have decided against deporting French Jews, but the police were still arresting French citizens who were in violation of regulations. Albert must have been using false papers to disguise the fact that he was Jewish and had been informed on. He was bundled into a police car. The city's landmarks were silhouetted against the night sky as he was driven to the red-brick Rothschild Hospital in the 12th arrondissement on the other side of the Seine.

The hospital still had doctors and nurses and patients, but had been turned into a prison as well, where people waited to be transferred to Drancy. The hospital had been founded by Baron Edmond de Rothschild in 1912. Maybe, during World War I, Albert had visited wounded comrades there. Now he would spend the long hot summer of 1943 in the Rothschild Hospital.

Not long after Albert's arrest, a copy of Pinto's report on Pierre was sent to General de Gaulle's Free French. Pierre was then invited to meet with de Gaulle's secret agents in their Marylebone office in Dorset Square. Their HQ was a large Georgian house that had previously been the headquarters of the Bertram Mills Circus. It was still a centre of charades. The upstairs rooms were full of French clothes, toiletries, and suitcases that were issued to agents before they left for France. The tatty pieces of paper in Pierre's top-secret file reveal that he was recruited not as an SOE agent, but by de Gaulle's Bureau Central de Renseignements et d'Action, the Central Bureau for Intelligence and Operations, known by its initials as the BCRA. He became de Gaulle's, not Churchill's, secret agent.

Pierre had arrived in London at the perfect moment. After the invasion of the Soviet Union had brought the communists into the Resistance, de Gaulle had moved to unify the different movements under the control of his envoy Jean Moulin. Moulin, however, had just been captured and tortured by Klaus Barbie. He had died on the way to a concentration camp in Germany. His death decapitated the pyramid command structure of the Resistance, which was now in danger of slipping out of de Gaulle's control as the communists gained ground. It was a crucial moment. An Allied invasion of France was in the cards. De Gaulle desperately needed to assert his authority. The introduction of the compulsory labour service in Germany, the Service du travail obligatoire (STO), in February 1943, had prompted thousands of young people to go underground. The

General had to rally them behind the Free French, before they fell under the influence of the communists.

De Gaulle decided to divide France into regions that were given numbers. To each he would dispatch a commander supported by a sabotage expert. These teams would unite and train the Resistance fighters, and after the invasion, create a new civil administration. De Gaulle's recruits were to be trained by Churchill's Special Operations Executive.

Pierre's SOE file contains various reports from a series of training schools, where he underwent a battery of physical and intellectual tests. There were courses in paramilitary commando training and the art of silent killing. At the first training camp, Special Training School 6 in West Court near Wokingham in Berkshire, Pierre made a good impression. He had "a good knowledge of weapons," and when it came to map reading, he paid careful consideration to the theory. He also paid close attention to the use of charges. Although he did not suffer fools gladly, Pierre was judged to be a good leader. The officer in charge of the course was keen to deploy him as soon as possible. The instructors found him "the best shot and best all-rounder." He played football and enjoyed sports. Then, as the course came to an end, something changed. The officer in charge wrote in his report that "in a few years I am afraid [Pierre] will be very fat, very prosperous, with a wife in one flat and a mistress in the other."

♣

In June, Eichmann dispatched one of his trustiest lieutenants, Alois Brunner, to France. Thirty-one-year-old Brunner had already worked with Eichmann in Vienna and Berlin. In the northern Greek port of Thessaloniki, he had just applied his administrative flair with startling results. In just six weeks, his team had deported

42,830 Jews in nineteen transports, destroying the largest Sephardi community in Europe, which had existed for over four centuries. Although 42,000 Jews had already been deported from France between April and June 1943, not a single convoy had left the country. Eichmann was keen to keep to the timetable drawn up at Wannsee, under which all of France's Jews had to have been deported by the end of the year. It was Brunner's job to fulfill the quota.

Brunner was a sadist with a genius for organisation. His arrival would hone the Nazi killing machine, which from now on would centre on Drancy alone. French police were no longer allowed to enter the camp, but would help guard the perimeters from small wooden watchtowers. In each sat a French policeman with a machine gun. From now on, deportations would leave from the nearby station at Bobigny, which was easier to access and fed quickly into the main east-west railway junction. It was also significantly less conspicuous than the main station in Drancy as it was located on a quiet road.

Yet just as Brunner was about to start the mass deportations, Laval and Pétain suddenly changed their minds. They decided against the denaturalisation of all foreign-born French Jews. Not because they wanted to save their lives, but because they wanted to do things their own way. If the denaturalisation commission withdrew a foreign-born Jew's citizenship, according to French law, they had no objection to their deportation.

As the sea sparkled in Nice's Bay of Angels, Edith, like the other Jews who took the evening air on the seafront, had begun to consider the possibility that deportation was a death sentence.

Then disaster struck.

The Allies landed in Sicily on July 10, 1943. In the weeks that followed, fewer and fewer Italian soldiers were seen on the streets of Nice. Two weeks later, Mussolini was toppled in a coup. The

Germans invaded northern Italy, seizing control of the regions of Piedmont and Liguria that border France. Alpes-Maritimes was encircled. There was a growing sense of panic, which Edith somehow managed to hide from Huguette—she has no memory of worried conversations and mounting unease. Before she returned to Lyon, Marion must have told her mother that she had to get false papers. She would have told her whom to contact.

At the eleventh hour, in the stormy humidity of late August, Angelo Donati, an Italian banker and philanthropist, hatched an extraordinarily audacious escape plan to take thousands of Jews trapped in Alpes-Maritimes to North Africa. A fleet of ships had been chartered using money smuggled into France by the Jewish underground. The Jewish resistance began to bring thousands of Jews into Nice in preparation for the departure. Soon, 25,000 desperate Jews were crammed into the city. Brunner was ready to pounce and was waiting in Marseille with a commando squad of twenty-five SS officers, many of whom had also been with him in Greece.

The announcement of the armistice that had been signed between Italy and the Allies on September 3 was delayed in order to give Donati time to put his plan into action. Yet, before the exodus had begun, on September 8, the chief of Allied forces in North Africa, US General Dwight D. Eisenhower, announced that an armistice had been signed. While the handful of Italian soldiers still left in Nice celebrated late into the night, crowds of Jews gathered outside the Italian consulate in the desperate hope they might be given a visa. Meanwhile, local officials and police, on the orders of the new *préfet*, Jean Chaigneau, were in their offices frantically destroying files that might help the Nazis identify Jews. Among them were lists of people entitled to ration cards. In schools, the registers mysteriously disappeared. In Cannes, the list of those entitled to ration cards held in the town hall was altered so that all Jewish-sounding names were replaced by French ones. Even if that list had survived in the Municipal Archives, it is unlikely that I would have found Edith's name on it.

Edith and Huguette were trapped.

CHAPTER 12

The Suitcase

At daybreak on September 9, a convoy of German tanks rolled eastward along the Promenade des Anglais. As the sun crept up in the sky, under the palm trees, silhouettes in the ochre uniform of the Afrika Korps looked out across the Bay of Angels. It was hot and the air was heavy. For Edith, the unthinkable had happened. The coast was teaming with German soldiers and the Italian army had disappeared.

The following morning in the bright sunshine, Alois Brunner stepped down from the train. He requisitioned the nearby pretty Belle Epoch Hôtel Excelsior as a transit camp. Brunner then went to the Italian consulate to requisition the paperwork concerning the Jewish population of Alpes-Maritimes. His men threatened the officials with revolvers but were politely told that the papers had been transferred to Rome. It was a lie. The officials had destroyed them. Brunner then turned to the police to organise the role they would play in the roundup. To his surprise, they too refused to cooperate. The Wehrmacht did not involve themselves in roundups in France, as they were wary of the possible public reaction, so for the first time, the SS were on their own. Nevertheless, the arrests began at half past three in the afternoon.

Brunner was confident that informers would flock to help him. The price for turning in a Jew was set at 100 francs, roughly €30, but there were far fewer whistle-blowers than he had expected. The premium was raised to 1,000 francs, and then to 5,000 francs, but still, very few people came forward. The *préfet*, Jean Chaigneau, observed in his official papers that although there was significant anti-Semitic feeling in Alpes-Maritimes, the arrival of German troops had turned prejudice into compassion.

Frustrated and angry, the SS became increasingly violent, barricading streets and dragging people from their hospital beds. Brunner then came up with a new method of catching Jews—mobile *physionomistes*. A physiognomist is a person who is good at recognising faces. Brunner believed it was possible to single out Jews by a passing glance from the back of a black Citroën. The physiognomists he employed were White Russian and Ukrainian émigrés, who had fled their homelands after the 1917 Bolshevik Revolution. They were deeply anti-Semitic and believed every word of *The Protocols of the Elders of Zion*, which had been forged by the Tsarist secret police in the 1900s to implicate Jews in an international conspiracy to overthrow the government and subvert Christianity. It was, however, not that easy to spot French Jews. As the photographs of Marion, Huguette, and Edith taken in the summer show, they were far from easily identifiable. Many Jewish women with curly hair had had it straightened at the hairdressers. Hundreds of non-Jews would be the victims of this haphazard army of detectives.

The White Russians were also in it for the money. Operating alone, they forced their way into rich Jewish apartments and hotel rooms to steal whatever they could from their victims before dispatching them to the Hôtel Excelsior. But this was a different world from the Paris of 14 months earlier. The Jewish underground was now armed and capable of fighting back. Many of the White Russian informers who worked for Brunner befell mysterious "accidents" at the hands of the Jewish resistance. Two leading *physionomistes*, Serge Mojaroff, a former Tsarist army officer turned garage owner, and Georges Karakaieff, were murdered. The Jewish resistance also sent small wooden coffins with threatening letters to known informers.

Despite the chaos playing out in the city below, life in Avenue de Béarn continued with a veneer of normality. Huguette had done so badly at school in the previous term that she had been called back early from the holidays to attend remedial classes. She had to pass a test to be admitted into the next year before the new term began on October 1. It preoccupied every moment of her day, and she channeled everything into her schoolwork to block out more frightening thoughts. Huguette says her mother seemed calm and unflustered. Edith really was a tough woman. It cannot have been easy to control her emotions as the crisis unfurled. Realising the danger that they were in, she made contact with the Jewish resistance. In an audacious humanitarian rescue mission, a team of forgers had been brought into the city to make hundreds of false documents.

On Wednesday, September 29, Edith went into the countryside to buy food, as she did every fortnight. The following morning over breakfast, she told Huguette that their false papers were ready. While she was at school, Edith would go to pick them up. Huguette says she was cool and collected but did not say exactly where she was going. Huguette was sitting in a stuffy classroom working on her French grammar when her mother was caught in a trap.

An informer had betrayed the forgers. Brunner's men were waiting to pounce. Edith was arrested and taken to the Hôtel Excelsior. When she was manhandled down from the truck, Brunner was probably watching from the balcony, as was his habit, as she was forcefully pushed into the large white hallway. It was crammed with people. A huge swastika flag hung down from the ceiling.

Edith spent hours waiting among the agitated and desperate crowd before she was called into a room on the ground floor. There she was interrogated by three SS officers. The atmosphere was brutal and violent. The Drancy camp physician, Abraham Drucker, a thirty-eight-year-old Jewish doctor, who had so far avoided deportation, had been transferred to Nice. Born in Czernowitz, then in the eastern Austro-Hungarian Empire, Drucker spoke fluent German. He was also used as an interpreter during interrogations, but in Edith's handbag was her genuine *carte d'identité* that said she was from Berlin, so she probably found herself alone in the room with the SS. The interrogations were terrifying. Drucker, who survived the war, said that the SS often pulled out their guns, hit prisoners, and stubbed cigarettes out on them. Brunner's men wanted the names of family and friends. There is no record of what Edith told them, but as they had her false papers, they would have had Huguette's as well. No doubt they slapped them down on the table in front of her. Edith was then told to hand over anything of value. Eyewitnesses say that Brunner pocketed the best pieces of jewelry that belonged to the prisoners and sent a pearl necklace to his wife. If Edith was wearing any jewelry, the Nazis stole it.

As the afternoon dragged on, there was no let-up in the steady flow of prisoners who passed through the wrought-iron gates. The Excelsior was hot and stuffy, even after the sun had set. Three hundred people were crammed into the tiny hotel. They sat slumped on the stairs and on the floor of the lobby. Edith waited in fear that Huguette would appear in the hallway.

When Huguette came back from school, her mother was not at home. As she did not have a key, she went to the cinema. It was a logical place to go. Nice had forty cinemas and they often showed double bills. Sitting in the dark for hours on end was better than looking lost wandering the streets. The film to see was *Le Corbeau*, a drama set in a small French town, where poison pen letters ruin the lives of the inhabitants. In the late afternoon, Huguette went back home, hoping her mother would be there. No one answered the door. The weather was warm, so she climbed into the house through an open window. She ate and then immediately fell asleep.

At midnight, the SS arrived outside the childhood home of the future Nazi hunter Serge Klarsfeld on rue d'Italie, not far from the Excelsior. Eight-year-old Serge was woken by the beams of the torches and voices of the SS shouting in the street. Klarsfeld says, "When Brunner's SS broke into our Nice apartment building, beating our friends and neighbours, from our hiding place I heard—and I hear it still—my friends' father shouting, 'Help! Help! French police—Help! We're French! Save us! Save us!'" Nobody came to save them. Serge and his sister were hiding with their mother behind a false partition at the back of a cupboard, which was hidden behind a rack of clothes, while his father, Arno, quickly made the beds. When the SS knocked on the door, his father let them in. Arno, a thirty-nine-year-old Romanian-born Jew, told them his wife and children were in the countryside. The SS arrested him. Arno had volunteered to fight in the French army in 1940.

Not long after, Brunner's men arrived at the house on Avenue du Béarn. Shouting and yelling, they banged furiously on the door, but the house remained silent. For once, fifteen-year-old Huguette's hearing difficulties were a help and not a hindrance. Incredibly she did not wake up.

The next morning, as she was leaving for school, she found the neighbours standing in the street waiting for her. They warned her that Nazis had been looking for her and that they would certainly come back. They told her to leave as quickly as she could. The tip-off was a small act of kindness, a fleeting little gesture that cost nothing—but it saved her life. Huguette turned around and went back into the house. In a state of shock, she realised that her mother had been arrested.

Edith had shown her where she had hidden some money in a drawer. She took the cash and went straight to the station to buy a ticket to Paris, which had to be bought the day before. As soon as she had bought it, she went to friends of her mother's whose name she cannot recall and begged them to let her spend the night at their house. She promised she would leave first thing in the morning. Reluctantly, they let her in.

Early the following day, Huguette went back to Avenue du Béarn. She was hastily packing her bag, when a man with a beret pushing a wheelbarrow knocked on the door. He told Huguette that her mother had been arrested and that she should pack a suitcase for her. He explained that he was collecting the suitcases for those who had been arrested. Terrified, Huguette did not ask any questions, and alongside the clothes, she added a knife and some of the food her mother had bought the day before. She has spent the last seventy-five years wondering who the man was—and if he ever really did give the suitcase to her mother.

After the war, Huguette tried repeatedly to find out exactly where her mother went to pick up the documents. She was unable to find any record of the address. Marion knew that an informer had denounced the forger. It was gossip that spread quickly in the weeks that followed, but she knew no more than that.

Trying to find out more about forgers operating in Nice in September 1943, I stumbled across a testament on the United States Holocaust Memorial Museum website, given by 69-year-old Jacques Marburger, in 1993. I had seen his name mentioned in relation to the Jewish underground group the Sixième, so I clicked on the link. In 1943, Marburger was 19 years old. He had been recruited by the Sixième in the summer of 1942. In the film, Marburger says that, in September 1943, he and his colleague, Jacques Weintraub, had taken rooms at 16 rue Guiglia, not far from the station. There they worked night and day making false papers. Weintraub, the 23-year-old Polish-born leader of the Young Zionists, was a seasoned member of the Resistance and exactly the same age as Marion. Just before Brunner's arrival, he had smuggled children across the border into Switzerland. A faint smile occasionally runs across Marburger's lips as he tells his story. He still revels in the deception.

One evening in late September, not long after dusk, Marburger says that he and Weintraub stepped out into the dimly lit street with a fresh batch of 250 documents wrapped up in a towel, among them Edith's and Huguette's. It is likely they were heading for a restaurant near Place Garibaldi to hand them over. Marburger says forgers never gave them out themselves. The moment the two young men walked out of the front door, they were picked up by Brunner's men. It was widely believed at the time that the informer was a female member of the Jewish resistance, who may have tried to save herself by currying favour.

Marburger and Weintraub were taken to the Gestapo headquarters in the luxurious Hôtel Hermitage, not far from Avenue du Béarn. The building dominates the Nice skyline. When they were briefly locked in a room alone, Weintraub seized the opportunity to hide the documents in the plush red sofa. After a short interrogation, at about eight o'clock in the evening, the two men were set free. Their false papers, like Marion's, had been issued by council officials and were genuine items, which tricked the Nazis. When they reached the gates at the edge of the lush gardens that surrounded the hotel, Weintraub decided to risk sneaking back into the building to retrieve the documents he had hidden, as he knew that if the Gestapo found them, they would round them all up in a trap. Weintraub was caught red-handed. Although he was tortured, he did not give anything away. On Israel's Ghetto Fighter's House website, there is a picture of Weintraub with his wife, Lea. He is dressed in a smart suit with a waistcoat. She is carrying a stylish handbag. They were a good-looking couple. Now, all Brunner had to do was use an agent to tell people the documents were ready. When they came to collect their papers, the SS arrested each of them in turn. The reason Huguette was unable to find someone who knew where the papers had been collected is that everyone who had gone to pick them up was sent to Auschwitz.

♣

In the warm winter Riviera sunshine, I drive up to the elegant hilltop suburb of Cimiez with Cathie Fidler. She is a volunteer from the Association pour la Mémoire des Enfants Juifs Déportés des Alpes-Maritimes, who have campaigned to have the names of deported Jewish children memorialised in their former schools all along the Côte d'Azur. Fidler's mother was also a Jewish refugee from Germany, and her father was an artist who had been born in Poland. They had settled in Nice in 1920. In 1943, they fled the city and had gone into hiding in the village of Roussillon in Vaucluse.

Just over the hill from the grand villas, Fidler directs me to a street of small, terraced cottages on a steep incline. I park the car and we knock on the door of Edith and Huguette's former home. It is a tiny house with a green door, on either side of which are two windows with green shutters that are firmly closed. No one is home. Another pointless journey like the one I made to rue de la Ferme is about to conclude, when suddenly, the next-door neighbour pops her head out. She is wearing pink fluffy slippers and grey jogging pants. Fidler explains our mission. The neighbour looks about eighty. Although she moved in long after the war, she knows the story that a Jewish woman was arrested in the street. She mentions this in a gossipy relaxed way, leaning on the doorframe. I can see she is totally unaware of the enormity of what she has just said to me. I am completely taken aback that a total stranger knows such an intimate fact about our family. Not even our close friends know anything about this. It is all too convoluted and complicated to explain. I am lost for words. I am grateful Fidler keeps the conversation going.

"The woman who was arrested left important papers behind," the neighbour adds, nodding knowingly. Images of the empty house flood into my head. I had never thought about what was abandoned in the flight. What papers? Surely Huguette had locked the door? How did the neighbours get in? Did the SS smash the door in? The thought of the neighbours' pilfering fingers picking through Edith's drawers unnerves me to such an extent that I wish this house had been an empty address with no secrets to divulge. I wonder where the contents of the house ended up—scattered around the district like the debris from an explosion. There is no time for musing, though. I push the idea to the back of my mind, as no sooner has the neighbour introduced herself as Madame Luciani, than she is joined by her friend from across the road, who has popped out to see what is going on.

Within moments we are all ushered into Madame Luciani's kitchen for tea and dainty pink cakes. As she sets the table, Madame Luciani tells me her house is identical to the one next door. The houses have two floors as they sit on the edge of a steep hill. They are small but cosy. There are two bedrooms next to the front door, and at the bottom of a steep staircase there is just one room with a kitchen along the wall. Outside is a small garden. The sun streams in through the windows. I can imagine Edith bustling about cooking

Edith and Huguette's former home in Cimiez, 2019.

dinner less than two metres away from where I am drinking tea. It is a stark, eerie feeling.

Madame Luciani was a small child in 1943. To my surprise, she is as keen to tell her story as she is to listen to mine. I am so wrapped up in my own business that I am startled when another painful tale is served up. I had wrongly thought she would have nothing more to add. Her parents, she explains, worked as housekeepers for a Jewish family in Nice. When the Germans arrived to arrest them, she was playing in the garden with their three-year-old daughter, who was her best friend. "The Germans asked if she was my sister," Luciani says as she pulls her cardigan tight around her, although the afternoon is still warm. "Why didn't my mother say she was her daughter?" she asks me. I am not sure why she thinks I will have an answer. I have no idea what to say. Luciani is clearly troubled by the memory.

A silence fills the room before Madame Luciani gets up to close the French window to the garden. Over the rooftops in the distance is the blue of the Mediterranean. "It was good you came," she says as she sits back down. "Stories like this need to be remembered," she adds, as she refills the teacups. I am not sure which story she is referring to—mine or hers. There is something very raw in the air. I think that this may be the first time she has talked about this.

The conversation then turns to the man with the wheelbarrow. "*Ah, oui! Oui!*" the ladies say in unison, waving their hands excitedly. There were people in the Jewish community that the Nazis allowed to collect suitcases for those who had been arrested, they explain. It was all part of the elaborate trick they played on the Jews to convince them they were being resettled. The man with the wheelbarrow would have taken Edith's suitcase to the Hôtel Excelsior, they tell me.

When I get back to my Airbnb, I send Huguette an email and a picture of the house.

She confirms this is where she used to live, but says nothing about the man with the suitcase or the forger Jacques Weintraub. The next day, I walk back up the hill to Avenue de Béarn. I look at the house from all angles. It is a pretty and surprisingly tranquil place. There are no echoes and absences here. It is warm and affirming. I call a taxi to take me to the Hôtel Excelsior about ten minutes' drive away.

♣

Not surprisingly, the hotel management is reluctant to advertise the Excelsior's history. The owners have refused to let the local council put up a plaque on the hotel, but across the road the municipality has erected a black memorial. It is hardly good for business to tell clients about the ghosts who might haunt this dainty-looking building. I gaze at the notice board by the gate. It shows pictures of the rooms and how much they cost. A night at the Excelsior is about €200. The rooms look garish and modern. It is as if, like the former Hôtel Terminus in Lyon, they are trying too hard to forget the past.

I walk quickly through the white hallway and straight out into the small, walled courtyard garden at the back. It is dominated by a large tree in the centre. There are chairs and tables for guests to enjoy an aperitif, but it is early afternoon and deserted. I look up at the back of the building. Yvonne Singer, a Romanian Jew, threw herself from one of the top-floor windows on the evening of September 30, 1943. She was severely injured when she crashed on the stone floor. Probably the same floor, from the look of it. Edith would have heard her fall and must have seen her lying on the divan in the hallway afterward. The past is all around you—but you cannot always feel its echoes and cries—the thud with which the young woman must have landed on the stone courtyard is in my head alone. The terror it induced on those sitting on the stairs waiting for the worst is in a parallel universe. Miraculously, Singer did not die. She was released and managed to survive her injuries, thanks no doubt to the guiding hand of Dr. Drucker. I go back into the hotel and stand in the Excelsior's cool, calm, white hallway, until the young woman at the reception interrupts my thoughts to ask if I would like a room. I decline, a little too eagerly for a stranger walking into a hotel. I do not want to share this story with her. I leave as fast as I can.

From the Excelsior, I retrace Edith's steps and walk across the square in front of Nice Station. Groups of prisoners left the Excelsior three times a week. As soon as Brunner had fifty Jews in the hotel, he dispatched them to Drancy. On October 2, Edith walked with eighty-four other prisoners, under the pretty frescoed ceiling of the ticket hall. Among them was the forger, Jacques Weintraub.

Serge Klarsfeld's mother was in the crowd of people who watched them being marched inside. Her husband signaled to her to get away as quickly as she could. Cathie Fidler has told me that local people wrote letters to the town hall to complain how badly the Jews were treated as they made this short journey. Travelers made their indignation clear. Some even hurled insults at the German soldiers, who did not understand what they were saying. No one managed to escape. Edith and her companions traveled in a third-class carriage, which was attached to the back of the main Nice-Paris train. The journey took forty-eight hours as resistance attacks had damaged the railways across the country.

⚜

The next day I visit the city archives to look at copies of the local newspaper *L'Eclaireur*. It is in a beautiful villa, which once had a large garden that is now covered in 1970s apartment blocks. Nice must have been far more beautiful in 1943 than it is today. The paper is an intriguing mix of small ads and dramatic news. I am the only person there. The archivist has nothing to do and is keen to chat. He is intrigued when I ask for a train timetable. I stumble in my badly accented French. He clicks about on his computer and soon comes over to tell me there was only one train a day that left Nice for Paris. It started in Florence in the early morning. If Edith spent forty-eight hours in the Excelsior and it took Huguette the same time to board a train, they must have traveled on the same one. I cannot believe it. The expression on my face mystifies the archivist and he asks why I wanted to know. I feel I have no choice but to tell him the story. His enthusiasm for his job is invigorated. He tries as hard as he can to find out some other titbits to help me, but the archives reveal nothing. For the record, the story of the Jews' departure was not reported in *L'Eclaireur*.

I walk back along the Promenade des Anglais. Although it is late January, the sun is surprisingly warm. The sea is a deep azure blue. As I stroll along the seafront, I realise that transferring eighty-four Jews to the station in front of a crowd of onlookers must have demanded intense security. Huguette is a tiny person. It must have been easy for a short fifteen-year-old to slip through the barrier and take a seat on the train. Huguette remembers clearly that no one asked for her documents, which was unusual. Klarsfeld has said that it was extremely dangerous to try to leave Nice, as everyone's papers were carefully checked. Maybe at this vital moment all attention was focused on the Jews in the final carriage and the discontented mutterings of the bystanders. As a mother, I like to think that Edith's presence somehow saved her daughter.

Many of the girls in Huguette's class who had gone back to school the day before were not so lucky. Simone Veil survived deportation to Auschwitz, but a plaque, placed on the lycée in 2005 by Cathie Fidler's association, remembers the sixteen pupils who were murdered there over a thousand miles away. They were:

Eliane Dana, born 12 January 1922 in Nice, deported on convoi 62.

Colette Ewselmann, born 9 May 1926 in Nice, deported on convoi 60.

Nicole Friedmann, born 2 March 1929 in Paris, deported on convoi 64.

Monique Jacob, born 2 September 1929 in Paris, deported on convoi 62.

Ada Jochwedson, born 14 September 1922 in Danzig, deported on convoi 60.

Isabelle Jochwedson, born 14 September 1925 in Danzig, deported on convoi 60.

Geneviève Latalski, born 24 October 1924 in Paris, deported on convoi 60.

Janine Lubetzki, born 25 July 1932 in Paris, deported on convoi 77.

Paulette Molina, born 7 December 1925 in Marseille, deported on convoi 61.

Huguette Nehama, born 21 August 1927 in Belgrade, deported on convoi 62.

Vivette Politi, born 24 April 1926 in Paris, deported on convoi 76.

Fanny Spatzierer, born 27 May 1926 in Breil sur Roya, deported on convoi 60.

Germaine Steinlauf, born 6 December 1932 in Nice, deported on convoi 68.

Annie Willard, born 22 February 1928 in Mulhouse, deported on convoi 69.

Huguette Willard, born 22 February 1925 in Mulhouse, deported on convoi 69.

Lilli Wohl, born 25 February 1926 in Leipzig, deported on convoi 62.

Huguette Nehama was born the same year as Huguette, so she must have been in her year at school. In France, pupils are allocated to a school year from January to December of the year in which they were born. The Nehama family had already fled into the mountains. At this point, they were hiding in the pretty village of Clans. When I get back to the Airbnb, I look again at the 1942 school photo on Veil's Wikipedia page. I wonder if Nehama is the girl with the curly hair in the front row. Looking her up on Google, I discover that she was in fact born in Thessaloniki in Greece and was deported on *convoi* 66, not 62. Nehama died in Auschwitz on January 25, 1944. The online search also reveals the uncomfortable fact that in 2019, the plaque was defaced by the neo-Nazi group Nice Nationaliste.

♣

Later that evening my husband arrives. The following day we walk in the hot sunshine up to the Jewish Cemetery on Castle Hill. A wall of names of those Jews who were deported from Alpes-Maritimes and murdered in the Holocaust is about to be unveiled. The moment we arrive, my husband rushes up to the wall to check if his grandmother's name is there. He smiles in a strange kind of relief when he finds it. He is happy to see she has not been forgotten.

Edith's name is one of 3,603 engraved on the wall. Among those attending are Serge Klarsfeld and his wife, the family of Simone Veil, and many who wear a yellow badge with a Star of David, below which is written "*Les Fils et Filles des déportées juifs de France, militants de la mémoire.*" Their personal crusade is to stop the Holocaust from being forgotten. The Sons and Daughters of Jewish Deportees from France was set up by Klarsfeld in 1979. The organisation has documented the crimes committed against the Jews and filed cases against former German and French officials, among them Bousquet. Many of "the sons and daughters" are now frail and old. They lost their parents in the roundups along the Côte d'Azur many decades ago. They have lived with the pain ever since. Some are the descendants of the people who ran the Duboucharge Committee, who were the friends of the Resistance leaders like the forger Jacques Weintraub, whose name is also on the memorial. People whose eyes scan the wall may never know that he was a Jewish hero, as brave as any partisan or ghetto fighter. His wife was pregnant when he was deported, but she carried on helping Jewish children escape to Switzerland and survived the war. The Resistance ripples through the air. The ceremony that follows is full of symbolism and emotion.

As we stand under the cypress trees and the blue sky, the lead violinist of the Nice Opera plays "Le Chant des déportés." The song was written in 1933, by German political prisoners, and was played at Simone Veil's funeral. Six candles for the six million victims of the Holocaust are lit, the last one by my husband. Bernard Gonzalez, the *préfet* of Alpes-Maritimes, gives a rousing speech against anti-Semitism and anti-Zionism. "This is a serious moment," he says. "Not a week goes past without an act of anti-Semitism being carried out in France." I think of his predecessor, Marcel Ribière, who was happy to help hand over the Jews in the 1942 roundup, and Ribière's successor, Chaigneau, who did everything in his power to protect them—even hiding Jews in his own apartment. The ceremony ends with a rendition of "La Marseillaise" to the accompaniment of the local fire brigade band. This is not just the singing of a national anthem, but an assertion of a set of beliefs, and an affirmation of what goes wrong when you abandon them. It is a lesson for local politicians everywhere. It shows how understanding the past can help to shape the future.

Edith was unlucky. There was nothing inevitable in her arrest, and she had done everything she could to protect herself and her daughters. The roundup was a failure, though. Brunner had hoped to catch at least 25,000 Jews in Nice, but arrested just 1,800. Brunner would stay in Nice until December 14, when he closed his operation at the Hôtel Excelsior and returned to Drancy. Brunner failed not only because ordinary people stood up to him, but also because Vichy officials finally refused to help. The Nazis did not retaliate.

CHAPTER 13

A Month in Drancy

It was late in the evening when Huguette's train arrived at the Gare de Lyon. During the journey, an inspector had checked the tickets. When he saw her *carte d'identité* that said she had been born in Berlin, he asked if she was Jewish. She said, "No," and he chose to leave it at that. Disorientated and frightened, Huguette then made her way to her father's apartment through the dark and empty streets. The capital's elegant buildings were draped in swastika flags. French traffic signs had been replaced by German ones, but there were hardly any cars. This was a city where the Jews wore yellow stars and were forced to travel in the last carriage of the Métro and the trams. When she finally arrived, it was after midnight. Johannes was shocked to see her and alarmed when she told him that her mother had been arrested.

When Huguette woke up the following morning, the sound of the clack of wooden soles that replaced the worn-out leather of people's shoes echoed on the pavements outside. Johannes had already left the apartment to get her false papers. He spent the days that followed brooding anxiously. He said very little to Huguette, who drew into herself. She has no memory of how his mistress Lucette reacted to her arrival. Huguette was in shock and has never been able to get over the fact that she was not able to say goodbye to her mother.

After Huguette had got off the train and all the passengers had left the station, the prisoners from the Excelsior were taken along the platform to a line of waiting buses. As they traveled through the empty streets, Edith looked out of the window at the city she had last seen three years before, and in which she had sought refuge ten years ago. She had no idea where she was being taken.

In the early hours of the morning, the bus finally pulled up in the courtyard at Drancy. The concrete five-story U-shaped building had never been finished. Prisoners crowded in front of the railings across the unglazed windows, watching. The SS guards yelled at the prisoners in German telling them to form a straight line. An internee translated. Edith stood for hours in the cold night air until it was her turn to be called into a busy office, known in Drancy as the Kanzlei, the Chancellery. The walls were lined with wooden filing cabinets that had been brought especially from Germany to hold the registration cards. A member of the Jewish administration, who were also prisoners, handed Edith a questionnaire to fill out. A clerk then recorded her civil status, the date, and the reason for her arrest on her registration card. Her remaining cash was taken from her and placed in a paper bag with a number on it. Edith was handed a receipt and told not to lose it. She was then assigned to a room. After she left, one of the Jewish staff filed the small index card away.

Brunner was so committed to his work that even after the Allied landings in the summer of 1944 he remained in Drancy planning deportation convoys. On the night of August 15, 1944, as a general strike began, there was feverish activity in the camp's office as his men stoked up the fires in the kitchens to burn the paperwork. In the confusion, the prisoners managed to hide vital documents in the cellar. The card index files were concealed under packages on a supply truck leaving the camp, among them Edith and Albert Haymann's, which were then hidden in a nearby butcher's shop.

In an ultramodern meeting room at the Mémorial de la Shoah in Paris, I meet Karen Taieb. She has spent over twenty-five years investigating the Nazi and French government paperwork that details how 76,000 Jews from France were murdered in the Holocaust. She shows me Edith's actual index card. It has a red border across the top on which a large capital "B" is written in thick black pencil. By the time Edith arrived at Drancy, Brunner had introduced a new system that categorised prisoners by three letters—A, B, and C1-C5. Category A was for spouses of Aryans and Jews with one Jewish parent. C1 was for camp personnel, who were the most privileged. C2 was allocated to Jews protected by their countries, such as Turks. It was a fragile protection and counted for little. C3 was allocated to the wives of prisoners of war. C4 was given to Jews waiting to be reunited with their families. They were used as bait and once the families were reunited, they were reclassified as B. C5 was for detainees who might be released if they could prove that they were not Jewish. Those assigned the category B were suitable for deportation as "eastern workers." The letter B was a death sentence.

The little index card shows that Edith was given an identity number—5939. Written on it, in fading pencil, are the bare facts of her life. Two figures below the red banner show she was imprisoned in stairwell 10, room 1. The housing complex was divided up into twenty-two different sections, each with its own stairwell. The Jewish prisoners who worked in the Kanzlei, Taieb tells me, were at that time digging an escape tunnel. It was only discovered when the sports hall next to the former camp was built in 1980. If Drancy had been emptied in a single night, Brunner would have become the laughingstock of the SS. The clerks were metres from freedom when Brunner's men caught them. They were deported on *convoi* 62. "The person who wrote this card most probably died in Auschwitz," Taieb says.

Nineteen-year-old Roger Perelman was arrested in Nice on October 24. Perelman, who was born in Poland, had been living underground since he had escaped from the Pithiviers internment camp in 1941. He had been arrested in one of the first roundups. In his memoir, *Une vie de juif sans importance*, he described Drancy as "a dirty, agitated, and noisy concentration camp." Internees urinated and defecated in the corridors, on the stairs, or in their rooms, as access to the toilets was limited. I pinch myself to remember this is a testimony of a man who survived Auschwitz.

When Edith walked into the room to which she had been assigned, she would have found, as Perelman did, "men, women, whole families, lying on the ground or on soiled straw, crushed by their fate, indifferent to the environment, to the promiscuity; individual hygiene was sketchy at best, and often overlooked." Bedbugs fell from the ceiling, and when she woke up on the cold concrete floor, she would have been disfigured by bites. The prisoners crowded around the new arrivals asking for news, and if they had seen relatives and friends. The atmosphere was feverish. The anxiety was heightened by the fact there was nothing to do but wait.

The day after Edith arrived in Drancy, at the daily roll call, a list of 1,000 names of "workers" who were to be sent to the east was read out. In agitation, some cried and shook with fear as they were led away to a separate stairwell. Before the convoy departed, there were numerous suicides. On October 7, the prisoners who had been selected for deportation were ordered down into the courtyard before dawn. Inmates crowded at the windows to watch. As they left, the deportees sang "La Marseillaise." From those who had been in the camp for some time, Edith would have discovered that this happened at least once a fortnight, and that most people did not spend a long time in Drancy.

The prisoners gave their destination a nonsense Yiddish name, *Pitchipoi*. Prisoners deported from Drancy who were selected for slave labour in Auschwitz were ordered to send postcards from Poland to their family and friends. They all followed an almost identical format: "I am in a labour camp and am well" or "I am healthy. Kisses." An identical trick was used at Treblinka, where Dutch Jews were asked to write postcards home without realising that in minutes, they would be dead. Although some people believed or wanted to believe they would be reunited with relatives who had already been deported, Perelman says, most people did not believe it.

Survivors said very little about Drancy, as the enormity of what happened in Auschwitz overshadowed the time they spent there. Yet, in the 1970s, Serge Klarsfeld, the eight-year-old boy who had hidden in a cupboard in Nice, had grown up to become a lawyer and a Nazi hunter. He scoured German newspaper photo libraries to find, and buy, as many photographs as he possibly could of the camp. He says it was "essential to show as clearly as possible the concentration camp conditions of this antechamber of death," where his father spent the same amount of time as Edith.

While her mother was in Drancy, Marion took an incredible risk. She tried to rescue her. She approached one of the police on guard at the camp gate and tried to bribe him. It was well known in Paris that the police in Drancy took bribes, especially if you had Christian birth certificates for the prisoner you wanted released. The policeman asked her what her mother's number was. Marion had no idea and could not believe that she could not be identified by her name. The only person who would have had that kind of documentation, and access to the money, was Johannes. They were both unaware that Brunner had instituted a new regime and there was now no way out of Drancy. Marion was lucky she was not caught. The French policeman told her to go away as quickly as she could.

How long Marion stayed in Paris I do not know, as Huguette has no recollection of her visiting. Her anger with her father must have reached a boiling point, and I am sure she quickly returned to Lyon.

On the evening of October 13, 1943, the French service of the BBC broadcast a programme called *The Hell of Drancy*. It warned French officials to be aware of the consequences of their actions and urged people to save the Jews, especially the children. By now many of the police assigned to Drancy were listening to Radio Londres. The broadcasts had an enormous impact and prompted many people to think twice about their own individual actions.

On October 20, Eichmann received a request for a train to be given permission to leave Drancy for Auschwitz eight days later. One of the first things my husband told me on our first date was that his grandmother had been murdered in Auschwitz, so I am not surprised when I see this document. What does shock me is that while searching on a French government website through the list of names of those denaturalised between 1940 and 1944, I discover that the day after permission for the deportation train was granted, Edith, Johannes, Marion, and Huguette were stripped of their French citizenship. Like a perfect storm, everything had come together. The denaturalisation commission had made their decision in May, but the decree had only been issued two weeks earlier. The reason for the delay is not clear. Although their address was given as rue de la Ferme, the authorities were now on the lookout for Johannes, Marion, and Huguette. Even though by now they all had false papers, it was an incredibly dangerous moment; since 1942, it was the law that when a person was denaturalised, they had to be presented with the decision in person at the *préfecture*, the town hall or the police station. Under German pressure, the denaturalisation commission had, the month before, begun to ask the police to track down those who were in hiding. The chance that Vichy officials might have intervened to prevent Edith's deportation had disappeared. There was no hope for her. It was the final betrayal. Edith would be deported as a stateless person.

♣

On an overcast October day seventy-six years later, my eldest daughter, Esther, and I arrive in Drancy. It is instantly recognisable from the photographs taken in the 1940s. It is scrubby, low rise, and down at the heels. My GPS tells me to turn right toward the former internment camp, which is moments from the high street. I park on a suburban road of small, early-twentieth-century houses. It is clear immediately that it would have been impossible for the people who lived here to have not known what was going on. The camp was literally on the other side of the road.

Three large middle-aged women in hijabs wait glumly with their shopping trollies at the ultramodern bus stop opposite the former camp. Esther and I cross the street. The suburbs, or *banlieues*, of France's 93rd department grew up around nineteenth-century factories conveniently situated at arms-length from the elegant Parisian boulevards. Even the weather is greyer here. In French, *banlieue* is often used as a pejorative term. For most Parisians, the 93rd is a world of decayed housing projects, crime, unemployment, and impoverished immigrants which is best avoided. It is a point of view that, in light of the story I am piecing together, leaves an uncomfortable feeling in the air. In the inter-war years, Jews were accepted if they assimilated and spoke French. Most of the Jews who were arrested in the Vél d'Hiv roundup were poor and lived on the margins of French society. Many of France's five million Muslims face discrimination and marginalisation. Today, forgotten by Parisians, Drancy and nearby Bobigny, two of the 93rd's *banlieues*, face a unique problem on top of the predictable—the challenge of remembering the past when the present is so fragile. It tells you as much about the present as it does the past.

Across the road from the bus stop is a large monument, beside which a French flag hangs limply against the steely grey sky. The monument is full of symbolism and references to Jewish culture and religion. It was designed by a former deportee, Shlomo Selinger, in 1976, but I find it seriously ugly all the same. In 1988, the year my oldest son was born, a freight wagon was placed behind the monument. Since then, it has been vandalised on numerous occasions. But despite the few metres of railway track that lead up to it, there was no station here. Holocaust commemoration is full of inaccuracies that feed the arguments of those who deny it ever happened. Where the wagon now stands was a barbed wire fence. Prisoners were taken by bus to the nearby railway tracks that delivered them to their deaths.

The name "Drancy" is engraved in the floor of the Holocaust memorial at Yad Vashem in Jerusalem. In the memorial's Hall of Remembrance, it has a worthy gravitas. Yet for a place so symbolic, Drancy is a surprise. The former concentration camp behind the freight wagon is a grimy, low-rise housing development, and for over 500 people, mostly immigrants from Africa, nearly all single or single parents, Drancy is home.

In post-war France there was a housing crisis, so the local municipality quickly completed the construction work, and, in 1948, the first residents moved in.

In the summer of 1943, Brunner ordered a driveway to be laid out that ran around a central lawn. It was planted in early October and watered with sprinklers. It still exists, an innocuous scrubby lawn that looks as if it was built for children to play on. The twenty-nine-square-metre studios where, in 1943, up to fifty people were held, are too small for families. There are now modern PVC framed windows, but little else has changed. The stairwells are dirty and the paint on the stairs is badly scuffed. Nearly all of the units on the ground floor that the architects intended to become shops, doctors' surgeries, and nurseries are boarded up. When you are allocated housing here, you are not told about the building's past. As Esther and I walk around the estate and up and down the stairwells, the strangest thing is that there is almost nobody about. What is clear is that the state of disrepair shows a callous indifference to the memory of what once happened here, but more importantly than that, a disregard for the lives of those who live here over seventy years later. There is no one around to ask what it is like to live in a former concentration camp, but it is obvious that if you end up here you have few choices in life. For many it is one step up from the street.

The three women are still waiting for the bus when we come back to the main road. Maybe Samy Amimour, a Muslim of Algerian origin, once drove the route. A local bus driver, he joined the Islamic State in Syria in 2013. In 2015, he came home and took part in the attack on the Bataclan nightclub in Paris that cost 130 people their lives. Radicalisation is an issue in Drancy, as it is in many poorer parts of the country. Drancy is a place that still retains a sense of urgency and the ability to expose the fault lines in French society.

The housing complex became a national monument in 2001, and a small museum, the Mémorial de la Shoah Drancy, opened opposite the estate in 2012. When it was built, local residents complained that the past was of more interest than their present problems. It was designed not to intrude on them and for visitors to look down on the former camp through large glass windows, a step away from reality. Next door is the hotel where, from the third-floor bedrooms, relatives and friends tried to catch a glimpse of their loved ones. The memorial's director, Jacques Fredj, said Drancy needed "a building that was neither flashy nor arrogant. A transparent place." He succeeded. There is a plaque the size of a paperback book by the entrance. It is so discreet that we miss it.

CHAPTER 14

The Rejected

On Monday, October 25, 1943, 1,000 internees with a *B* on their card index were summoned into the neat, newly laid-out courtyard in Drancy. Prisoners crowded at the windows to watch as Edith stood in the pouring rain. She was placed in a group with fifty other prisoners. They would travel together in one wagon on the train.

As they clustered together on this wet and windy morning, two people who spoke German were appointed to be the *wagonführer*, the chief and deputy chief of the group. Edith would not have been given the job, as Brunner liked to appoint fathers, who were less likely to condone escapes if their families might be shot in reprisal. Scouring the archives, I read eyewitness accounts of the deportation. As a result, I discover Edith was told to collect her suitcase, the one that Huguette had hastily packed and given to the man with the wheelbarrow, and move with the group to stairwell 9. I can now answer Huguette's question about whether her mother ever got the suitcase, not that it makes this story any easier.

701 MIIHAUD Jean	14.6.26	Student	6694	
702 MISRAKI Michel	13.12.97	Büreauangestellter	6199	
703 MISUL Alfred	8.4.77	Zeitungsverkäufer	6861	
704 MODAI Alegra	11.9.02	ohne	5865	
705 MOISE Roger	2.3.06	Ingenieur	6205	
706 MOISI Jules	3.7.02	Bauleiter	6843	
707 MOLINA Georges	16.11.81	Kaufmann	6427	
708 MOLINA Louise	5.1.90	ohne	6428	
709 MOLINA Paulette	7.12.25	Studentin	6429	
710 MONTEUX Jean	3.7.89	Angestellter	6224	
711 MOREL Erna	19.9.23	Sekretärin	6131	
712 MORGENSTERN Séhia	3.9.02	Elektriker	6633	
713 MOSES Marcel	14.9.06	Vertrauensmann	6081	
714 MOUFLARGE Estella	31.10.27	Schülerin	6731	
715 MUHLSTEIN Arnold	27.9.28	Schülerin	6130	
716 MUHLSTEIN Bernard	2.8.99	Kaufmann	6128	
717 MUHLSTEIN Mina	23.11.98	ohne	6129	
718 MULLER Edith	18.3.98	ohne	5939	
719 NAHMIAS Isaac	8.9.06	Kaufmann	4263	
720 NAMENWIRT Eva	28.4.24	ohne	6045	
721 NAMENWIRT Hélène	20.9.27	Studentin	6046	
722 NAMENWIRT Hersch	6.10.94	Seelensorger	6043	
723 NAMENWIRT Riwka	Apr.1893	ohne	6044	
724 NAMER Henri	15.8.14	Buchhalter	6225	
725 NAQUET Cadette	30.9.17	Studentin	7056	

List of passenger names from *convoi* 61, including that of Edith Müller, number 718.

On the card that Karen Taieb had shown me at the Mémorial de la Shoah, a clerk had crossed out the number of her room 10.1 and written 9.2. This is the room where she would have spent the nights before the deportation. The tiny slip of card records the moment she was condemned to death. Taieb had also found a yellowing piece of paper that recorded that Edith had arrived at Drancy with 1,864 francs in her purse. It was a page from a little copybook that shopkeepers used to use with stubs and receipts. The money, an average amount according to Taieb, was confiscated when she arrived in Drancy. In the days before their departure, each person assigned to the convoy was called into the Kanzlei. The paper bag that held Edith's cash was taken out and placed in front of her. The money was recounted before she was handed a receipt for the amount in Polish zlotys. She was told she would be able to reclaim it upon her arrival in Poland. It was a trick Brunner had already used successfully in Thessaloniki. When I saw the receipt, I wondered at first if it had been in the pocket of Edith's coat that she would have left on a peg in the undressing room in Auschwitz. Then I realised that she probably did not even have a coat, as the day she was arrested it was warm and sunny.

It was still dark, when the following Thursday at five thirty in the morning, the prisoners on stairwell 9 were ordered down into the courtyard. Roger Perelman was among them. He later wrote that Brunner was himself present. In fact, at that very moment, Brunner was in the mountain village of Clans arresting Huguette's classmate, Huguette Nehama, her family, and the sixty-six other Jews hidden in the locality. As they stood in the courtyard in Drancy, the prisoners were told that they were being transported for work and would be reunited with those of their families who had already been deported. Surrounded by old people, nursing mothers, and small children, Perelman found it difficult to believe that they were being sent east to work. Did Edith's eyes scan the rows of prisoners or was she too afraid to look up? What went through her mind? Huguette thinks she was constantly looking around her, checking that she had not been caught.

Simone Veil, who was deported the following year, wrote in her memoirs: "No one had heard of Auschwitz and I had never heard the name mentioned. How could we have the first idea of the future the Nazis had planned for us? It has become difficult today to imagine the extent to which information during the occupation was rationed and compartmentalised; the police and censorship saw to that." I hope that Edith was unaware of what awaited her. Veil was, however, a fifteen-year-old girl, and Edith was an avid listener of the BBC, but when you do not know what horror is possible you can still hope. Perhaps Edith thought that they needed workers in the east to cook and wash clothes for the Germans. Edith was, after all, only forty-five years old. She was young enough to start a new life.

Each of the prisoners was allowed to keep the few belongings that they had brought with them to the camp. The suitcase that Huguette had packed for her mother was with her as she boarded one of the twenty familiar green-and-white buses on loan from the Paris Métro waiting in the courtyard. The prisoners were loaded onto the buses in the same groups of fifty they had been allocated to the previous Monday. They were driven to the station in Bobigny by regular uniformed drivers, who gave the genocide a mundane and reassuring look. This was French complicity in action.

The train was waiting by the platform. It had arrived from Germany the day before. It was made up of twenty-three freight wagons and three passenger cars. That evening, a group of female prisoners had been ordered to clean the filthy wagons, which were used to transport coal and all kinds of other cargo. The twenty Sipo-SD policemen from Munster, who would escort the train to Auschwitz, were standing on the platform with ferocious dogs on leashes. In charge of the team was a man named Schramm. I try but cannot trace him. The prisoners were lined up in front of the wagons in rows of five, one after the other. Perelman says that they were violently herded on board by the guards with whips.

When we met at the Mémorial de la Shoah, Karen Taieb gave me a photocopy of the convoy dispatch documents that were immediately sent to Eichmann in Berlin and to Auschwitz. According to Brunner's instructions, the list of deportees was organised alphabetically. As they stood in the courtyard at Drancy, they were grouped accordingly. Each prisoner is listed by name, date and place of birth, and profession. Edith was prisoner 718. The lists of the names of those on the deportation convoys, like so much of the vital evidence of this horrific crime, were found by the lawyer Serge Klarsfeld, whose father's name is further down on the list. The document says that also on the train, but in a separate wagon, were 3,500 kg of honey, 4,500 kg of potatoes, 275 kg of sugar, 80 kg of ersatz coffee, 275 kg of pasta, 250 kg of margarine, 350 kg of salt, 275 kg of dried vegetables, 500 kg of canned vegetables, 1,919 kg of grapes, and 15 kg of chocolate. The figure for the grapes is so specific, I wonder what would have happened if one less kilo had arrived in Auschwitz. Typed below the list of goods is an instruction that reads, "I ask for these high-quality foods to not be given to the concentration camp prisoners." As if they are potatoes or dried vegetables, it then says that if the exact number of 1,000 Jews is not delivered, Drancy would like to be informed. The tight, tiny, cramped signature of Alois Brunner is on the bottom right-hand side of the paper. I spend a long time looking at it.

On arrival at Bobigny, each busload of fifty people was allocated to a freight car. Counting down the neatly typed list of the prisoners' names, I can see that Edith probably traveled in wagon 13. To my astonishment, I can then identify the fifty people with whom she took this last journey, and with whom she spent the last days of her life. Sixteen of the pupils from the Lycée de jeunes filles in Nice were deported to their deaths. One of them was in wagon 13.

Paulette Molina was two years older than Huguette. Maybe Edith recognised her? Perhaps she was friendly with her mother, Louisa, who was also in her wagon and knew her from parent's evenings and the school gate?

Convoi 61 pulled out of the station at ten thirty in the morning. It took three days to reach Auschwitz. The train was crewed by staff from the SNCF, France's national, state-owned railway company. It drove through Noisy-le-Sec, past the champagne vineyards of Épernay, on to Châlons-sur-Marne, Revigny, Bar-le-Duc, and Novéant-sur-Moselle, which had been renamed Neuberg after the Nazis had annexed Alsace-Lorraine. The Gestapo paid SNCF 18 francs per kilometre for the use of the track via a German travel agency based in Place de l'Opéra. It was 336 kilometres to the border, and the overcrowding in the wagons was an economic necessity. There was not enough room for everyone to sit on the floor.

In France, there was not a single attempt to sabotage a deportation convoy transferring Jewish prisoners. It was the deportations for forced labour in Germany that had the biggest impact on French society and prompted popular active resistance. Most railway workers never encountered the seventy-nine Jewish deportation trains or those that transferred Jews internally within France. The convoys nearly always took the same route, so the same railway men, in the same stations, would have been the only ones to have seen what was happening. The two-man crew only arrived at Bobigny station after the SS had closed the doors of the train. The unarmed drivers were accompanied by heavily armed Germans. There was no question that any intervention would have had life-threatening consequences. Nevertheless, in Lille, one SNCF worker, Marcel Hoffmann, saved forty Jews from deportation—many of them children—and was recognised as Righteous Among Nations. Most of the help offered was not enough to earn anyone such recognition, but it does not mean that small acts of kindness should be dismissed. Some railway workers smuggled water onto convoys. German reports also show that others were accused of helping Jews to escape by slowing down the trains at crucial points during the nighttime, especially when they were near a forest. Other workers loosened the floorboards in the wagons. The SNCF staff often picked up the hastily scribbled notes which had been slid through the cracks of the freight cars as they passed through the stations. They often forwarded them on to families and loved ones. Yet, the option remained to simply throw those notes away if you had no empathy with the people being deported. Some staff even gave them to the Gestapo, who then arrested their loved ones.

Two days into the transport, a young woman, Lisa Kouchelevitz-Rosenblum, threw a letter from the train. Her words provide a strikingly accurate prediction of what was about to happen: "I have no more strength to cry . . . they will finish us up. We are here 1,000 people. Among us are many old people and small children. Where they are going to take us, we do not know." Unlike the formal letters written by anti-Semites, the denunciations and those written in protest at the treatment of the Jews that were all carefully thought through and neatly written in ink, these letters were scribbled in desperate haste. They are the final sound of the voices of the missing. Kouchelevitz did not survive. Many of the notes thrown from the train must have disintegrated on the tracks in the rain and snow. Perhaps Edith tried to write a few final words that were never found.

At Novéant-sur-Moselle, not far from Metz, the SNCF crew was replaced by one from the German Reichsbahn railways. When the deportation trains stopped, the SS walked up and down along the platform issuing warnings that anyone who tried to escape would be shot. The train then crossed the German border. It is often claimed that there was an escape in the tiny station at Bar-le-Duc on October 28, but it occurred on a deportation convoy of political prisoners that left the same day from Compiègne heading for Buchenwald. Perelman says, "Any escape seemed impossible: we had not been able to find the tools necessary to open the floor, the window of the wagon was very small, the *chef de wagon* rushed at us at each gesture that seemed to him suspicious, and it would have been necessary to 'neutralize' him to escape." Throughout the journey, he says there was no difference between day and night. "We were standing, sometimes sitting, hardly ever lying down; without being able to sleep, and moreover without sleep: the anguish, the cries and the tears of the little ones, the promiscuity, kept us awake." After the second day there was nothing to drink.

Convoi 61 arrived at its destination in the middle of the night. The train stopped in the Oswiecim freight station at the *Alte Judenrampe*, the old Jewish ramp, about a third of a mile from Birkenau. Trains only began to pass under its red-brick gate in the spring of 1944. As the doors opened, searchlights with powerful projectors shone into Edith's face. Her eyes would have blinked in shock after days in darkness, as the cold frosty night air swirled into the stinking compartment. The train's whistle made a continual screaming sound as she stepped down onto the wide concrete ramp. The prisoners were told to line up in rows of five. A loudspeaker announced that they had arrived at Auschwitz Workcamp. Perelman recalled that "men in striped pyjamas rushed forward." They shouted in a mixture of Yiddish and German that all baggage had to be left on the train. The women were immediately subjected to a selection and those loaded onto lorries were driven directly to the gas chambers. Late on the night of October 30, Edith was sent to join a long queue of people standing in the freezing cold. It is likely she stood there for some hours unaware of the significance of the smoke and soot raining down on her. The men were similarly selected and made to wait until early in the morning of October 31, by which time the women who had gone to the chambers were all dead.

Edith's suitcase was taken to the sorting room. Maybe it is one of the 3,800 suitcases that survive in the museum at Auschwitz. Prisoners at camps as far away as Stutthof on the Baltic Sea were made to mend shoes that were of good enough quality to be sent back to Germany. Edith's shoes would have been smart and elegant. Did the woman who later stood in them know their story? What happened to Edith's hair? Did I see a strand in the display case at Auschwitz and not even know? The plan was that she would disappear without leaving a trace. In a strange coincidence, Marion would die on the same night, October 30, sixty-seven years later.

From the convoy of a thousand people, only forty-three survived. Just three of them were women. Perelman had been arrested with false papers under the name Skoutelski. At the Mémorial de la Shoah, Karen Taeib showed me his Drancy registration card. If he had not been selected as a slave labourer when he arrived at Auschwitz, he would have died under the name Skoutelski, and no one would ever have known what had happened to Roger Perelman. It is a chilling thought that haunts me while I read the original list of those on the convoy that was drawn up by Brunner's men—were they all who they said they were?

♣

Back in Drancy, when I key "Gare de Bobigny" into my GPS, Esther and I are expecting to find a modern station with a small plaque. A sanitised memory that you take a photo of for Twitter and then leave. To our surprise, however, I am instructed to park on a busy main road next to some dilapidated but inhabited caravans that are surrounded by empty cans and excrement. A small, steep staircase hidden by the trees leads down to the original Bobigny station that was built in 1928, but the gate at the top is padlocked. The doors of the building down below are bricked up and the windows boarded. All we can do is stare down at it from the bridge over the railway tracks as the traffic thunders by. In 1943, the Route des Petits-Ponts was a quiet tree-lined street.

There are a series of information boards on the bridge overlooking the tracks that describe how 22,453 Jews were deported from here between 1943 and 1944. It is impersonal. How could you know who they were? In 2016, the Bobigny council announced a €2.5m renovation project to transform the site into a major Holocaust memorial. Museums can make history easier to deal with. Seeing Bobigny like this is bleak and raw. It is like a slap in the face. The new memorial has since opened and is arranged symbolically with trees and plants from the Mediterranean and Eastern Europe. It is one of those ideas that sounds good in a council meeting, but leaves me cold.

Months later, on what would have been Edith's birthday, my husband is flicking through his Twitter feed over his morning coffee when he suddenly sees his grandmother's face in a post from @AuschwitzMuseum. They post pictures of victims every day on their birthdays, so if we had thought about it before, there was a certain element of inevitability about this. In astonishment, he sits straight up in bed. He quickly regains his composure and retweets the post, saying: "It's amazing to see this pop up. It is my grandmother. She is not forgotten." Over 55,000 people like his tweet. It gets even stranger when people began to write, "Sorry for your loss." Huguette is the only person alive who remembers Edith. "You cannot grieve for someone you never knew," he says. He is right. Grief in the conventional sense is not the legacy of what happened for the rest of us. Brunner plunged a knife into Marion and Huguette's family. That wound has healed, but like scar tissue, it can suddenly feel uncomfortable, even raw and painful.

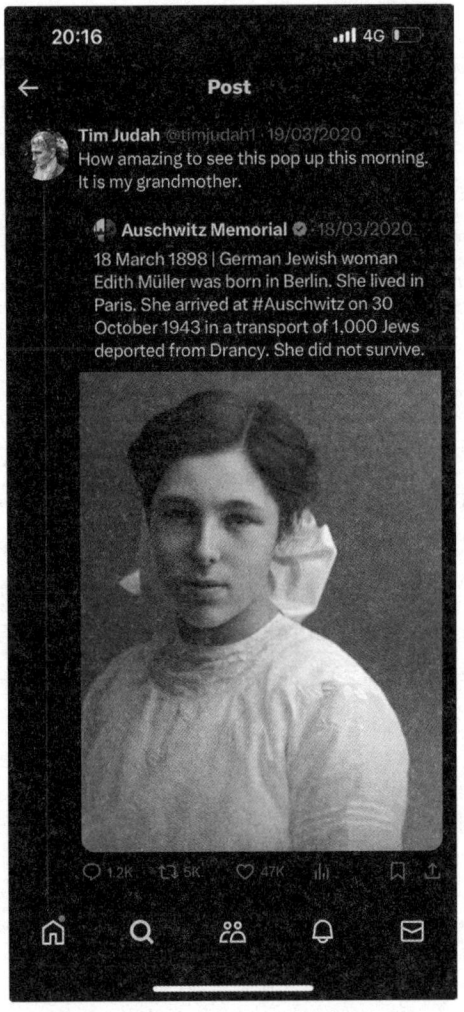

Photograph of Edith Müller on the Auschwitz Memorial Twitter feed, March 19, 2020.

The picture that has gone viral is the one in a small silver frame that I found hidden in a suitcase in Marion's box room. The Auschwitz Twitter feed took it from the Mémorial de la Shoah's online archive, where one of our nephews had uploaded it. The copy we have is faded, and I have often thought that one day there will be no picture left to see—but suddenly, a man on Twitter colourises the picture. It is a very kind thing for him to do, but it is unnerving all the same. Neither my husband nor I know what Edith's exact hair colour was, nor the colour of her eyes, but a total stranger has decided this for us and the image is now doing the rounds on the Internet. Why did social media followers like Edith and give the tweet such unprecedented traction? Why click "Like" on one stranger's face and not another's? People search for redemption in stories like this, but there is none. The only message from Edith's story is that evil exists, and we must always be on the lookout for it. If 55,000 people had protested at Bobigny station, it might have made a difference. I say this to a friend, who says no one could have done anything as they would have all been shot. Twenty SS men could not have shot 55,000 people if they had stormed the train, but it seems that is the way we like to think it would have been. It absolves us of any responsibility.

CHAPTER 15

The Killer

In November 1943, Pierre returned from a training course to a damp and stuffy London. Jean Moulin had been put up in a hotel in De Vere Gardens near Kensington Palace, not far from where Marion would live after she moved to England in 1961. It is possible Pierre stayed there, too. A browning piece of paper in his SOE file says that, as Lieutenant Plumeau, he signed the Official Secrets Act in Horse Guards in Whitehall. Written at the top of the page, in thick pencil, is the querying "Haymann?"—his real name. Pierre spent two weeks in London, but even with the Free French, he had to watch his back. Among those who had made their way to Britain, who frequented the French House bar and restaurant in Soho and who staffed the BCRA headquarters, were many former members of *L'Action française* and even the extreme right-wing terrorist group La Cagoule.

While Pierre waited for his next orders, on November 11, his father, Albert, was transferred from the Rothschild Hospital to Drancy. It had been twenty-five years since the armistice that ended

World War I. Albert's arrival followed the same pattern as Edith's six weeks earlier. He was allocated to a room on stairwell 19. His card in the camp files was also marked with the letter "B." Marion had nothing but scorn for Albert. After Pierre had left the country she had gone to Paris, at his request, to tell his father that he must leave the city. He had told her he had nothing to fear as Napoleon had emancipated him.

As his father waited in Drancy, Pierre caught the train from London to Manchester to start his second training course at RAF Ringway, now Manchester Airport. His report says that he remained "very cheerful and was the life of the party." He passed with a third-class after four parachute jumps. The following day, Albert was among a group of prisoners assembling in the courtyard at Drancy. The French authorities were not informed about the departure of *convoi* 62. Albert was exactly the type of person for whom they would have intervened to protect him from deportation, if he had been lucky. He was descended from generations of French Jews, a veteran, and an old man, but that chance was taken away from him. Like Edith, he would step on board one of a series of buses that took him to Bobigny station. Albert was forced aboard the freight wagons with 1,200 other people, of whom 150 were children. This time, a hundred people were pushed into each of the twelve wagons. Once the doors were sealed, the guards seated themselves in the passenger carriage behind the steam engine. In charge of the deportation was a Schutzpolizei staff sergeant named Friedrich Köhnlein, whom I have failed to trace.

The train followed the same route as *convoi* 61, but on an uphill part of the track the engine slowed down, probably deliberately to let the prisoners escape. Nineteen men from the first wagon fled into the darkness and dense fog. Among them were some of the clerks who had dug the tunnel in Drancy. Köhnlein reported back to Berlin that, after the escape, all the male prisoners had their shoes confiscated. Albert walked barefoot from the *Alte Judenrampe* to the Birkenau camp, where he queued in the freezing cold until it was his turn to be gassed.

♣

Brunner's cramped signature on the deportation documents haunts me. I download his photograph onto my desktop and sit and stare at his face—the face of a killer.

It is a black-and-white headshot taken in 1942 when he was thirty. On the surface there is nothing out of the ordinary about Brunner at all. He has small, expressionless eyes, bushy eyebrows, and thick lips. His dark hair, although it does not look like it in the photograph, was said to be wavy. His looks reflect the Central European melting pot into which he was born. He is far from an Aryan pinup. My oldest son tells me that I have developed an obsession, and eventually, when I can no longer bear the picture on the desktop, I put it in a folder—but Brunner cannot simply be forgotten and filed away.

I am nagged by the question of why a young man from rural Austria would decide to devote his life to killing people he had never met who lived thousands of miles away. My son is right; it becomes an obsession during the COVID-19 lockdown. I end up reading two books about him in German (painstakingly, on Google Translate). Then, as soon as I can, I visit the small village of Rohrbrunn where he was born.

The moment I get out of the car I am almost run over by a lorry and momentarily wish I had never come. But what turns people into fanatics is an important question. For Brunner, it all began at the tiny River Lafnitz, a picture-perfect bubbling brook just outside Rohrbrunn that in 1918 became the border between Austria and Hungary, which cut the German-speaking population of the village off from the town of Burgau, now a four minutes' drive away. It left a lasting mark on the young Brunner, who was forced, until the border was redrawn in 1921, to go to a school that taught all lessons in Hungarian, a language he could hardly speak. It hot-wired into him a passionate German nationalism. According to his biographers, he learned his anti-Semitism at the kitchen table and in the local church. Not that at this stage Brunner had ever met a Jew; the nearest Jewish community was in the town of Gussing, about eighteen miles away.

In the cemetery on the hill above Burgau, we find the graves of the Brunner family. It is unnerving. Brunner had the luxury of knowing where his family was buried. It was something he denied tens of thousands of families.

After the war, Brunner went into hiding and died in his own bed in Syria. He was a strange Nazi in hiding, as he gave interviews to the press boasting about how proud he was of what he done. He once said, "My only regret is I didn't murder more Jews."

What does my passing obsession with Brunner reveal? That most leading Nazis were not arrested and never faced trial. It is one of the reasons that we know very little about perpetrators and why they committed genocide. Serge Klarsfeld, the little boy who had hidden behind the partition at the back of the wardrobe in Nice, and his wife, Beate, did everything they could to track Brunner down and bring him to justice. But he died peacefully in his own bed. Most Nazis did. Their crimes are chronicled in endless books as a warning from history, but it was how the world reacted to them that was the real lesson. When the disinterest of the war years faded and the evidence was examined, it was accompanied by a misplaced acceptance of the inevitability of evil.

That is what Huguette asked me to challenge when she suggested that the young doctor in Val d'Isère, who offered to help her at the direst moment in her life, should be recognised as Righteous Among Nations.

PART V
THE SILENT VICTORY

CHAPTER 16

Looking for Dr. Pétri

Just weeks after her mother was deported, Huguette came home from school and told her father she had overheard some girls in her class gossiping that she must be Jewish. That must be why she had just turned up in the middle of the term. Johannes decided in a split second that there was to be no more school for Huguette—and that it was far too dangerous for her to stay in Paris. He ordered Huguette to leave immediately for Lyon. From now on she would live with Marion. It is possible he wanted to get rid of her, but while Marion had been in Paris in October, they may well have discussed a long-term plan. As she did not trust her father, Marion probably thought Huguette would be safer with her. Paris was a dangerous place; now that they were denaturalised; the police were looking for them. Whatever the reason, nothing was explained to Huguette.

When Huguette knocked on the door at 30 Montée du Gourguillion, she expected to find Pierre at home with Marion. Marion said nothing about him having left for Spain. She would have had no idea if he had made it to London. So, she simply batted the question away, saying he was just out of town. Huguette remains adamant that he was living in Lyon. Through the Resistance network Marion must have had a rough idea of her mother's fate, even if she did not have the full details, because she only allowed her sister to stay one night in the city. The local Gestapo chief, Klaus Barbie, and the Vichy paramilitary police, the Milice, were intensifying their hunt for Jews. Jumping over the platform barrier at Lyon station because they had not bought a ticket the day before, Marion and Huguette leapt onto the train and fled the city. They made their way high up into the mountains to Val d'Isère. Surrounded by towering peaks and dense forests, it was then one of the remotest villages in the Alps.

Although before the war Val d'Isère had begun to develop into a ski resort, in 1943 the village was still home to just 150 people. Its hotels provided the perfect cover. Marion told Huguette they were on holiday. Still in shock, Huguette believed her, and until our trip to San Francisco in 2019, she never thought to question what her sister had said. It was likely that Marion went regularly to Val d'Isère to collect ration cards for people with false papers. She also said on more than one occasion that she had taken people up into the mountains so they could try to cross the border. She never said anything about this to Huguette. Marion never changed her story, and more than once pretended that Huguette had broken her leg during the Italian occupation, probably to deflect any other questions we might ask.

In fact, Val d'Isère was never occupied by the Italians. In 1940, the French defences on the Col du Petit Saint-Bernard had been breached. Bourg-Saint-Maurice, Séez, and Sainte Foy at the lower end of the valley were annexed by the Italians. As in Nice, the civilian population suffered under the occupation and resentment grew. The Italians did not cut off Val d'Isère and the nearby village of Tignes completely, but the Italian customs demanded a tariff from everyone crossing the border of 150 francs, about €50 in today's money. The only alternative was to take the dangerous mountain paths. Nevertheless, Val d'Isère was an enormously risky place for Marion to take her little sister. Once Mussolini was toppled in July 1943, the Italian troops disappeared overnight. Not long after, the entire area had been occupied by the Wehrmacht's 157th Reserve Division, who had just been relocated from the Russian front. They had orders to track down fugitives, partisans, and smugglers. German soldiers were based in Val d'Isère's Hôtel Glacier and the Hôtel Solaise. It was the Gestapo, however, who called the shots. Their headquarters was in the Hôtel du Petit-Saint Bernard in Bourg-Saint-Maurice, but Gestapo officers were also based in the Hôtel de Mont Pourri in Tignes. The Germans knew that thousands of Jews and young men and women who were trying to evade being drafted to work in Germany were hiding out in the Alps. The soldiers pillaged the hotels and restaurants and burned chalets to the ground if they found someone who had been drafted to work in a German factory and failed to show up. Men from Val d'Isère who had joined the partisans were captured and taken to the notorious Montluc prison in Lyon. Jews who were caught were transferred to Drancy. Those who had hidden them were sent to concentration camps or simply shot. Locals still refer to the occupation as *la terreur*.

It was against this backdrop that Huguette slipped and broke her leg. The break was so bad that when Dr. Pétri saw the injury, he said that she needed to be taken to the hospital. The moment he said this, Marion punched him in the face. The Gestapo were watching the hospitals for wounded members of the Maquis resistance fighters and Jews—that punch was a cry of utter desperation. Marion was an incredibly calm person who never raised her voice, and for her to do something like this is an indication of the immense stress she was under.

Huguette's question still remains—why did Dr. Pétri risk his life for a total stranger?

On a genealogy website, I discover that Dr. Pétri went on to become the mayor of Val d'Isère, welcoming royals and celebrities to the slopes, among them Princess Anne and the Empress of Iran. Pétri was thirty-nine when he took Huguette in. Tanned and athletic, he looked much younger. There are photographs of him skiing in his shirtsleeves.

Dr. Frédéric Pétri skiing in his shirtseleeves in Val d'Isère, c. 1945.

The web page is hosted by a Christel Pétri, whom I message immediately on Facebook. Christel is Dr. Pétri's daughter. I tell her the story of Huguette and her broken leg. She replies that her father never mentioned to anyone, not even his wife and his children, that he had hidden and nursed a Jewish girl during the war. She is not surprised he kept quiet, she adds. In Val d'Isère, no one ever spoke about what happened during the war because the response to the German occupation had divided the community. As a result, even the families who still live there today have no idea that members of the French Resistance operated in the town. I arrange to meet her at her home in the foothills of the Alps.

It is raining heavily as my husband parks the car outside Christel's wooden chalet in a small village not far from Chambéry. Low clouds swirl over the hills. It is almost exactly seventy-six years since the events that link us together. Christel ushers us into her sitting room and toward her large wooden table. She has her computer ready. She is writing her own account of her father's life. The manuscript is open on the desktop. Before we start to talk, she goes off to make coffee, which is strong and welcoming.

As the rain batters on the windows, Christel explains why she is not surprised that her father helped Huguette, even though "to hide a Jewish girl there was a very dangerous thing to do. The house was also his surgery and was on the main street." We had always imagined that the chalet was hidden in a dense forest. Christel grew up in the chalet that had two floors and a garage for her father's red Bugatti. "My father was driven by a passion, not for plastering broken legs, but for caring for people," she tells me. At medical school in Strasbourg, he had specialised in psychiatry. "He had an unwavering sense of altruism," Christel explains. "He was profoundly generous and all his life he did everything he could for other people. He had inherited from his family, which had a long Protestant lineage, humanist values that guided every moment of his life. His father had taught him that every man is responsible for his choices and what he does with his life."

Miep Gies, who sheltered Anne Frank and her family, echoed these words when she said, "My decision to help Otto [Frank] was because I saw no alternative. I could foresee many sleepless nights and an unhappy life if I refused. And that was not the kind of failure I wanted for myself. Permanent remorse about failing to do your human duty, in my opinion, can be worse than losing your life." That remorse was what haunted Madame Luciani in Nice when she asked me why her mother had not said that her best friend was also her daughter.

Pétri lived with his mother, who was a widow, and his sister, who had her own apartment on the first floor. "In the winter he made his house calls on skis," Christel says. The family also had a couple of rooms that they rented out to guests, which Pétri sometimes used for his patients. It was here that Huguette spent much of the dark days of the winter of 1943–44, alone with strangers at the top of a mountain, not knowing what had happened to her mother. She says that Dr. Pétri came every day to sit with her. He listened to what had happened to her, asking questions and offering words of comfort, although the sense of loss and the all-consuming fear that Huguette must have felt was not something he could cure. What is clear is that the doctor had a big influence on the way she viewed the world. He showed her it was not an entirely dark place, and that is the reason that I am now drinking coffee with his daughter. I have yet to tell Christel that Huguette is hoping her father will be recognised as Righteous Among Nations by Yad Vashem. It is such a difficult process that I do not want to disappoint her if the request is rejected.

Christel has a picture of her grandmother on her computer. Madame Pétri is a motherly looking lady with horn-rimmed glasses, her hair swept back in a bun. Christel explains that she did all the cooking, and she is wearing a pinafore in the picture. Life was hard in the mountains that winter, but the Pétri family shared everything they had equally with Huguette, even pasta that was smuggled over the border from nearby Italy. This is crucial evidence for the Yad Vashem commission, which has asked specifically how she was cared for. Nor did the Pétris ever ask for any money, not that Marion and Huguette had any to give to them. It is important that the rescuer never sought to profit from their actions in any way.

Madame Pétri and her daughter looked after Huguette and brought her meals to her room. She spent hours reading. Christel has a cousin, Elizabeth, who was twelve years old in 1943. She suffered from tuberculosis and spent a lot of time in Val d'Isère. She helped out by taking the breakfast to guests and patients, but, during the winter of 1943–44, she was told that she should never go up to the top floor of the chalet where there were two rooms. Under no condition was she allowed to enter the room that looked out over slopes behind the chalet. This room was later Christel's bedroom. "It was the perfect place to hide someone as it had a small window facing the mountain," she says. "Nobody ever went behind the house in winter as there was a risk of avalanches so if she had a light on no one would have seen it." Christel thinks that they were worried that her cousin might tell the children she played with in the village that there was stranger in the house and someone might inform on them.

Christel is surprised that Marion had chosen to hide in Val d'Isère in the first place, but thinks the answer might lie in why her father originally came to the village. In 1938, Pétri, who was passionate about winter sports, was escaping a failed marriage. He decided to join his friends, world-class ski champions, who had founded the resort a few years earlier. Like many of the young men who ran the hotels and ski schools, Pétri had been born in Alsace, a region of eastern France that before World War I had been occupied by the Germans. The region was governed directly from Berlin and a policy of Germanisation alienated the population, who were proud of their French heritage. French was banned and Frédéric Pétri was christened Fritz, a name that stuck. The Pétri family was fiercely anti-German and their father insisted that only French be spoken at home. It was an important lesson. At the kitchen table, Dr. Pétri had learned how it felt when there was no acceptance that people are different. In 1919, Alsace was returned to France under the Treaty of Versailles. Hitler later renounced the treaty, and as the 1930s wore on, the possibility that it could be seized back by Germany became a fear that turned into a reality in 1940.

Pétri was a close friend of Charles Diebold, who had served in the Germany army on the Russian front in World War I and had learned how to ski. On trips to the Vosges mountains, he introduced Pétri to the sport. Pétri was soon an accomplished skier. He went on to do his military service in the Alps and was stationed in Tignes. Diebold moved to Val d'Isère in 1932, where he opened the first ski school. In 1938, he persuaded Pétri to join him. A year later, war broke out and Pétri was mobilised. Left alone in Val d'Isère, Pétri's widowed mother and sister, who had joined him in the mountains, found themselves on the front line as the Italians occupied the valley across the Col de l'Isèran. The village was evacuated, and the villagers were only allowed to return after the armistice. Pétri was taken as a prisoner of war to a camp in Germany, where he remained for eighteen months. In the camp he took tremendous risks caring for prisoners with tuberculosis before the mayor of Val d'Isère made an appeal for his release, as there was no doctor to care for the sick in the entire valley. A Jewish doctor named Azoulay, who was hiding out in the valley, stood in for Pétri whenever it seemed safe for him to do so. Dr. Pétri finally arrived home in November 1942 just before the Italians occupied the Haute Tarentaise.

When the Germans occupied Val d'Isère in September 1943, a resistance network soon developed that crisscrossed the mountain passes. One member of the group was Germain Mattis, a local ski instructor who was arrested by the Germans in June 1944. He died in a concentration camp at the age of twenty-seven. Pétri was not an official member of the Resistance, Christel explains, as it was too dangerous for leading members of the community to do this. If they were caught, the Nazis would carry out revenge killings, but Pétri, the priest Marcel Charvin (known as the "skiing curate"), and the mayor Nicolas Bazile were all sympathetic to their cause. The leader of the Resistance was Marius "Mario" Chabert, the local teacher. He also worked as the secretary in the town hall, which in the 1940s was in the same building as the school. With Bazile's blessing, he gave Jews and evaders of the STO false papers (see page 112, bottom) and ration cards. Marion must have known this. It is the reason that she trusted the doctor and left Huguette in Val d'Isère.

After Marion left, the situation in the Alps became increasingly dangerous. In the run-up to the Normandy landings, partisan activities grew exponentially and provoked severe reprisals. What Marion did and where she went, she never told anyone, but she seems to have stayed in the mountains.

When my middle daughter, Rachel, was ten, she went on her own to have lunch with her grandmother. As she served up the oven chips, Marion suddenly told her that once she had been hiding in a clearing in the woods with a group of other people. She had gone to fetch water with an unnamed person, and when they returned to the clearing, they found that everyone had been murdered by the

Nazis. Before Rachel could ask a question, Marion got up and went into the kitchen; this event in her life was never mentioned again. My husband was in Baghdad at that time, covering the ground invasion of Iraq. Why Marion had said this to Rachel mystified me, but then upon reflection I realise she was trying to show her that war is not as abnormal as it might seem. There was no need to have a huge discussion about it. She simply wanted to show Rachel that her grandmother had also been there. There was nothing unusual about war and you had to learn to live with it. Not long after, Marion gave Rachel a book, *La Résistance expliquée à mes petits-enfants* by the well-known Resistance leader Lucie Aubrac, who had been a major player in the Resistance in Lyon. She handed it to her without any explanation. It was just one of those clues that Marion sometimes left lying around, as if she would like someone, someday, to work out that there was more to her than simply being a housewife. I wonder if at this point in the war she had been with one of the brothers of the two boys who were arrested in the Vél d'Hiv roundup.

To my surprise, before we leave, Christel tells us another interesting tale about her father. The village was liberated in August 1944, but the local resistance network carried on the fight in northern Italy, which was still occupied by the Germans, supporting the partisans across the Col de l'Isèran, the highest mountain pass in Western Europe. Once again, Dr. Pétri would place his life on the line for a total stranger. On a freezing cold winter's evening in November 1944, Pétri set off to help rescue thirty-nine British soldiers who had escaped from an Italian POW camp. As they were being led over the mountain pass by the partisans, they became trapped in a snowdrift. They were not dressed for the winter weather and were freezing to death. When Pétri finally found the soldiers, only one of them, Alfred Southon, was still alive. He was barely breathing, but Dr. Pétri refused to give him up for dead. He carried him back to his chalet and, with his mother's help, cared for him until he was well enough to leave. Christel explains that this was a potentially unpopular move, as many people resented what they saw as Britain's abandonment of France at Dunkirk and the bombing raids on French cities. Just as Dr. Pétri had said nothing about hiding Huguette, he did not mention this adventure to the rest of his family either, until Southon became a celebrity in the UK. After his story was told in a 1953 BBC radio documentary, Southon made a return trip to Val d'Isère. This is an important piece of information for the Yad Vashem commission, because the Righteous Among Nations often carried out more than one attempt to save a life. Most rescuers regarded what they had done as completely normal and never felt the need to talk about it.

Hoping to learn more about resistance activities in Val d'Isère, I send several emails to the town hall and local radio station. When I was emptying out Marion's flat after her death, alongside her false papers I found a black-and-white photograph of her standing between two men with skis propped up beside them. She looked radiant but extremely tense. My sister-in-law told me one of the men might have been a pharmacist who was in love with her and, after Pierre left, had wanted to marry her. She says that one of the men must be him. I post the picture on a local Facebook group and explain why I am asking for information.

I get just one reply, and surprisingly, it is from a member of the famous Paris hairdressing dynasty—Roby Joffo. He is the nephew of Joseph Joffo, the author of the Holocaust memoir, *A Bag of Marbles*. We meet at his flat in Paris the following month. He is a musician with a large quiff of white hair. Roby's father, Albert, and his uncle Henri, Joseph Joffo's elder brothers, were, he tells me, also lying low in Val d'Isère during the winter of 1943–44. Their father had been deported with Albert Haymann on *convoi* 62. They felt secure

Marion in Val d'Isère, c. 1942–44.

enough in Val d'Isère to work in a hair salon on the main street opposite Pétri's chalet. Roby is a bit of a ladies' man and jokes that his father may have cut Marion's hair, especially if she was a pretty woman. He has seen the picture. *A Bag of Marbles* is a classic that all my children read at school; I am shocked that the Joffos have a connection with Marion and Huguette, however tenuous. After the war, his father and uncle returned to Val d'Isère and bought the salon. Joffo remembers Pétri well, and says that the families have remained friends. Roby is adamant that there were other Jews hiding in the valley. Christel has told me that some of them had joined the local partisans. Joffo makes several calls to Val d'Isère, but nobody seems to know anything about it. He was clearly not expecting such an eerie silence and looks baffled. The conversation comes to an end. He promises to stay in touch, and, although we become Facebook friends, for the moment that is that.

♣

After we leave Christel's house, my husband and I drive up to Val d'Isère. As we climb up the valley, the first snow of winter is falling. I am dreading this part of the journey. I am irrationally convinced that the car will skid, and we will both die. Today, when you reach Tignes, the road passes along the edge of an artificial lake, which did not exist when Huguette was hidden here. Below the water is the old village of Tignes. This valley is a fickle place. It gives with one hand and takes away with another. Just across the dam in the tiny cemetery is the grave of our nephew Jeremy, Marion's eldest grandchild, the son of François, her second child with Pierre. In 2004, Jeremy was forced into the water of the nearby Lac de Tignes by an avalanche and drowned. Like his grandparents, he loved the mountains. If Marion had told anyone the story of what happened here during the war, it would have been Jeremy. This loss is still raw.

When I step out of the car in Val d'Isère, there is thick snow on the ground. Today, it is one of the world's most famous ski resorts. Modern buildings stretch along a narrow mountain plateau. All the original chalets are long gone. It seems rather soulless. The Pétris' chalet was the last to be demolished and has been replaced by a block of flats that belongs to the family. The hair salon where the Joffo brothers once worked is now a boulangerie. I leave as fast as I can. I do not like this valley at all. It is, I feel, still a dark place.

When I arrive back home in London, I email Huguette the news that I have found the Pétri family. She agrees that it is time for us to write to Yad Vashem to ask if they would consider recognising Dr. Pétri as one of the Righteous Among Nations. After I lodge the application, I try to arrange an interview with the then-mayor of Val d'Isère, Marc Bauer, to ask him to comment on the possibility that Dr. Pétri might be recognised as Righteous. When I get no response by email, I telephone the town hall. Down the line, a member of staff tells me it is not possible for the mayor to comment, as this is a "delicate matter." Gobsmacked, I wonder what could be so delicate about honouring one of his predecessors.

Years ago, I watched Marcel Ophuls's 1970 documentary, *The Sorrow and the Pity*. Set in Clermont-Ferrand, it shows how the war had divided France and left deep cuts that remained raw. The film shattered the myth that de Gaulle had spun that France had been a nation of resisters and only a handful of people had collaborated. It showed the French as cowards and timeservers, people who change their views according to the prevailing circumstances. The film was so controversial that it was banned from being shown on French TV until 1981. I cannot believe that France is really the same today. I need advice and turn to an academic. The war divided communities, explains Jane Metter, who researches the period at London's Queen Mary University. For those who collaborated and those who resisted, "the only way to carry on living with your neighbours after the war was to forget what had happened." For Dr. Pétri to have hidden Huguette was, she says, "a 100 percent dangerous thing to do" and an act that would not necessarily have been applauded after the liberation, either, as "the region was a highly Catholic, conservative, right-wing society." The archives in Annecy, not far from Val d'Isère, are full of letters written to the authorities during the war, often anonymously, denouncing people for acts of resistance. The history of World War II still haunts France. Marcel Ophuls would have known instantly why the mayor of Val d'Isère thought this was a delicate issue.

Yet again, it is clear that despite the thousands of books, documentaries, and feature films about the Holocaust, this is a story that is still evolving and there is still much to be learned. Huguette's decision to revisit the darkest period of her life offered Val d'Isère a chance to address its past. At first, it seemed it was not an action the resort was ready to take. Then, I wrote a story about Dr. Pétri for BBC Online. The piece received more attention than anything I have ever written, even though everyone in the family besides my daughter Rachel thought no one would be interested in reading about Huguette and her broken leg. One Londoner who has a holiday property in Val d'Isère, whose mother was saved by the Kindertransport—the rescue of thousands of Jewish children from Austria, Czechoslovakia, and Germany, organised by the British Jewish community just before the outbreak of the war—started to raise money in the resort to put up a tree in Dr. Pétri's honour, with a plaque next to it explaining what he had done. When he approached the mayor for permission, he was told bluntly that the mayor did not believe that the story was true. The town hall's reaction caused such an outrage that I was invited onto the BBC Radio 4's flagship lunchtime news show, *The World at One*, to tell the story. It was a surreal moment, but one that showed the power of stories like Dr. Pétri's.

CHAPTER 17

Jews with Guns

Three months after Huguette broke her leg, Pierre finally made his way back to France. On a moonlit night in March 1944, he floated down by parachute into the Languedoc highlands east of Castres, in southern France. With him was Bernard Schlumberger, codename Droite, a thirty-two-year-old Protestant from Alsace. He was to be the Free French envoy, the *délégué militaire régional*, in the Toulouse region of southwest France. Pierre, now using the alias Tarare, possibly after a town near Lyon, was his explosives expert and right-hand man. At Special Training School 17, SOE's "Finishing School" for saboteurs, Pierre had been taught how to blow up trains sky-high.

It had been fifteen months since Pierre had left France, and the country was now more dangerous than ever. On New Year's Day 1944, Laval appointed the head of the Milice, Joseph Darnand, as the Secretary of State for the Maintenance of Order. France was to be liberated with blood and fire. The Milice shot dead members of the Resistance on the street and left the bodies as a warning. The *délégués militaires régionaux* were Gestapo targets and were also hunted down by the Milice. As they were volunteers, secret agents were not covered by the Geneva Conventions. Schlumberger and Pierre were parachuted in to replace a team that had been arrested by the Nazis. Schlumberger had visited a dentist in London, where a cyanide pill had been hidden in a detachable filling in one of his teeth. The agents' brief was to unite the scattered local resistance militias behind de Gaulle. Their base was to be in the tiny town of Vabre, where, in return for cash and arms, they had been guaranteed protection by the leader of the local partisans, Guy de Rouville. The mission was fraught with danger. Pierre was used to the shadowy world of the Lyon underground, but, within the Resistance, there were substantial regional as well as social differences. The wild hills of the Languedoc were perilous unknown territory.

In the depth of the night, Pierre and Schlumberger retrieved their kit bags and radio and hid their parachutes in the bushes. They then set off on foot through the rugged mountainous terrain. The following evening, as Odile de Rouville, the wife of the local Resistance leader, sat sewing by the window in Vabre, she saw two silhouettes run toward the house. Moments later there was a knock at Odile's door. A tall young man walked in and said, to her surprise, "Hello, cousin." This family tie was the foundation stone in de Gaulle's new forward operating base and key to the two agents' safety. It was no accident that Schlumberger, a Protestant, had been paired with Pierre.

Vabre, a greystone town on the banks of the fast-flowing Gijou River, was a Protestant village with Protestant partisans. The Maquis de Vabre took their name from the French word for the southern scrubland, where many such groups operated. Pierre was the link to an exclusively Jewish armed militia group, the Compagnie Marc Haguenau, who were camped out in the Gijou valley. Schlumberger and Pierre would merge the two groups together. Within weeks they would become part of the Free French Forces—the Corps Franc de la Libération, known by the acronym, CFL 10. A plaque in Vabre marks the spot where Schlumberger first met the leader of the Jewish partisans, Robert Gamzon.

Gamzon was far more than just a military commander. He was a man with a philosophic mission. Before the war, he had been one of the founders of the Jewish scout movement that wanted to take France's urban Jewish population back to the land and train them for a kibbutz life in the Palestine Mandate. Gamzon's company were not only Zionists, but they were also observant Jews who dedicated the Sabbath to prayer and kept a kosher diet. Gamzon saw celebrating Jewish identity and Zionism as the key to their survival. After the war, many of Gamzon's Jewish partisans would help survivors to make their way illegally to British-controlled Palestine. Although Pierre could not have been less like Gamzon if he tried, the two men would build a crucial relationship and Pierre's skills would be quickly passed on to Gamzon's men.

Before he began to train the Compagnie Marc Haguenau, Pierre traveled 400 km to Lyon to find Marion. It was a risky thing to do, as the SS and the Milice were on the lookout for him. When they were reunited, Marion dyed Pierre's hair red to disguise him. This was one story she loved to tell, because as she did so she joked that they would one day have a baby with red hair. The paramilitary police, however, soon tracked Pierre down. Despite all the checks before he left London, a woman in the laundry recognised that his shirts had been made in Britain and reported him to the Milice. There was a shoot-out, in which Pierre was injured. He managed to escape by jumping from a window. The couple then hurried to safety in Vabre.

From Castres, Pierre and Marion took the single narrow-gauge railway, which was controlled by the partisans, up into the wooded valleys that surrounded the town. He led her along a steep dead-end track through the forest to Schlumberger's HQ. The path was guarded at key points by the Maquis. Eventually, on the brow of a hill, a large stone farmhouse came into view. Next to the house was a wide field with breathtaking views across the valley. It was ideal for parachute drops. It was here that Pierre and Marion would run out in the moonlit to gather up the explosives, weapons, and money that fueled their battle against the Nazis.

Marion always said that the people of rural France were insular. She said they disliked anyone who was not from their locality, both Jews and Germans alike, and wanted them to just all go away. It was a sweeping statement that was not entirely true. The story of how the people of the village Le Chambon-sur-Lignon saved the lives of thousands of Jews has been well documented. The 5,000 residents mounted a rescue mission and hid between 3,000 and 3,500 Jews in the village and surrounding countryside. In 1990, the entire town was recognised as Righteous Among Nations, but it was far from the only place heroic rescues happened.

Vabre was no different. The town was a secure fortress, where for a moment Marion could breathe easily. Although they were reunited at last, it is likely that Marion was often left alone, as Pierre spent time away with the Maquis. He was a man of action, and in London they had judged him to be something of a loner.

♣

As I drive along the empty road toward Vabre, the trees form a leafy tunnel above the car. Fast-flowing streams cascade down the hillsides. At first glance, Vabre seems remote and isolated. It is still a largely Protestant place with a tight-knit community. It has just one café and one restaurant, but it is, and was, far from insular. The rivers of the Languedoc hills had fueled its industrial revolution. In the nineteenth century, tanneries and mills had sprouted up on the riverbanks. Life in Vabre revolved around the weaving business that belonged to de Rouville, the leader of the Maquis. The cloth produced in Vabre was sold to Jewish tailors in Paris. After the Vél d'Hiv roundup in the summer of 1942, de Rouville's Jewish clients began to make their way to Vabre on the miniature railway which was the last leg of the journey here, in the hope of finding somewhere to hide. In the 1940s, the railway network in France was far more extensive than it is today. Little railways like this were crucial as they helped Jews to make their way into the wild countryside.

Once the Jews arrived in Vabre, de Rouville and the local pastor, Robert Cook, organised hiding places in the isolated farmhouses and hamlets that dotted the forested hillsides. Cook was a staunch opponent of the Nazis. While a student in Paris, he had met Professor Karl Barth, a Swiss theologian who campaigned against Hitler and his followers. Immediately after the armistice, he and de Rouville had set up a local scout movement to protect the young people of Vabre from the influence of the Vichy youth movement. There was a strong unity in the local leadership, and the mayor Pierre Gorc issued the Jews false papers.

News of the help the locals had offered the Jews soon reached the Sixième, the Jewish resistance group that had tried to help Edith get false papers. They contacted Pastor Cook and asked him to hide thirty Jewish girls from Czechoslovakia, Germany, Hungary, and Poland who could not speak French. The children had been smuggled out of the internment camps at Rivesaltes and Gurs. Cook did not hesitate. He took them to a tumbledown farmhouse, Les Rennes, on the outskirts of Vabre. There they spent two months in hiding pretending to be Protestant refugees before the Jewish underground managed to take them across the border to safety in Switzerland.

Seventy-year-old Michel Cals, a former professor of literature and communications at Nice University, has, since he retired, returned to his hometown, where he has spent years researching the story. He is also an activist. In 2015, his campaign led Yad Vashem to recognise Vabre as a Village of the Righteous. "The Protestants of Vabre were outsiders in a predominantly Catholic country," he explains. On the edge of the town is a large building that is still known locally as the barracks. It was here that Louis XIV's soldiers were billeted during the persecution of the Protestant Huguenots—ancestors of the modern population—in the seventeenth century. Cals says, "The people of Vabre had not forgotten how the state mistreated their forebears and that is one of the reasons that they did everything they could to help the Jewish fugitives."

In August 1942, the police in Vabre were sent to the nearby spa resort of Lacaune with orders to put foreign-born Jews who were interned there under house arrest. Ninety were taken into custody, among them twenty-two children. All of them were later murdered in Auschwitz. The gendarmes from Vabre returned home in tears, and police chief Hubert Landes decided it was the last time he and his men would follow that kind of order. A year later he would warn Jewish refugees of an impending overnight roundup, urging them to hide. In 2021, he was recognised as Righteous Among Nations, thanks to a campaign led by Cals. "Landes's story," he says, "shows that every policeman had a moral choice and an option to not blindly follow orders."

The road to Lacaune cuts through the forest of chestnut, beech, and oak trees on the banks of the Gijou. In 1944, the mountains were so remote that the Germans were incapable of controlling the area. Short of men, they were only able to send out patrols from their base in nearby Castres. The valley is dotted with farmhouses and hamlets. After the roundup, Jews were hidden in the thick of the forests, where they created their own Maquis. The locals also made space for the Jews in their cemeteries. In the tiny village of Viane is the neatly fenced grave of Gilbert Bloch, one of the leaders of the Compagnie Marc Haguenau. He was killed in action in August 1944. "He had no family to claim his body. His father had died before the war and his mother had been deported to Auschwitz," Cals explains, "so he was buried here." In Lacaune, there is a collection of Jewish graves. They belong to elderly people who remained in the town after the liberation. They were the sole survivors of their families and had no one else to bury them. As we drive from hamlet to hamlet, Cals is greeted by residents who are all working on a new project to commemorate the valley's history.

From Lacaune, Cals drives up a steep road to wide-open moorland with commanding views. This was the site of another key parachute drop field known as La Virgule, the Comma. After Schlumberger and Pierre's arrival, this crucial lifeline was put under the command of the Compagnie Marc Haguenau. It was of vital strategic importance to the Allied war effort, as not only did it sit at the heart of the protected fortress of the Gijou valley, but it could be reached by planes flying from both Britain and territory under the control of the Free French in North Africa, which was by now General de Gaulle's base.

Cals runs a small museum in Vabre dedicated to the local resistance. It is home not only to Schlumberger's radio set, on which he received their orders from London, but also to a mass of paperwork from the period and testimonies from the men who fought in the Maquis. In the Maquis register, the names of local men are jumbled up with those of Jews born in Paris, Alsace, and Eastern Europe. It is evidence of a remarkable unity.

Archives that relate to the BCRA, General de Gaulle's secret service, are still embargoed in France because it went on to become the Service de documentation extérieure et de contre-espionnage, the External Documentation and Counter-Espionage Service. It was France's external intelligence agency until 1982 and played an important role in the war in Algeria. To my surprise, one of the box files in the wooden cupboard that holds Cals's archive includes reports from the period and messages sent by Schlumberger that would normally be classified. The documents reveal that Schlumberger's strategy was to concentrate on railway sabotage. It put Pierre centre stage. The extensive railway sabotage Pierre carried out in the region prevented vital transports of coal leaving the Carmaux mines, and the destruction of telephone cables reduced the Germans' ability to communicate.

The training that Pierre gave the Compagnie Marc Haguenau led them to carry out a dramatic attack on a German supply train heading for Castres on August 19, 1944. In a fierce shoot-out, the Compagnie suffered severe losses before the Germans finally capitulated. The *maquisards* asked their German prisoners, "Do you know who we are?" German soldiers were shocked when each of their captors announced, in German, *"Ich bin ein Jude!"*—"I am a Jew!" Gamzon and his men then went on to take part in the liberation of Castres, where they took a further 3,500 German prisoners.

There are pictures of them standing on the top of captured German trucks. The Jewish partisans then marched through the town singing the "Hatikvah," which, a few years later, became the Israeli national anthem. They would become part of the 12ème Régiment de Dragons and left Castres to carry the fight all the way to the Rhine.

Schlumberger's unit also included another Maquis group with a significant Jewish presence, the Montagne Noire's Trumpeldor platoon. They were named after the Zionist activist, Joseph Trumpeldor, who became a hero among Zionist groups after he was killed defending the settlement of Tel Hai in 1920. The group was also known as the Blue and White, as its members had what would

The Compagnie Marc Haguenau during the liberation of Castres, August 19, 1944.

become the flag of Israel sewn on the epaulettes of their uniforms. They were made by Jewish tailors from Paris hidden in the locality. The Trumpeldor platoon's uniforms also sported the lion of Judah and the Tabernacles.

Internal rivalries were a constant problem in the Resistance and challenged the authority of de Gaulle's *délégué militaire regional*. One of the most important men in the southwest region was the regional resistance commander Serge Ravanel, a member of the movement Libération Sud. He deeply resented Schlumberger's arrival. A Parisian Jew, he joined the Resistance in Lyon in the early days and had worked distributing newspapers and pamphlets. It is highly likely he knew Pierre and that their relationship smoothed relations between Schlumberger and Ravanel. At first Schlumberger, under orders from de Gaulle, refused to arm the entire Resistance, which included communists. Ravanel, the local commander, had many communists and Spanish Republicans under his command. In June 1944, when the Maquis de Vabre joined the Forces françaises de l'intérieur, Schlumberger agreed to be placed under his command.

Immediately after D-Day on June 6, 1944, Pierre was sent to train a Maquis farther north. His replacement was arrested and shot dead on the roadside before he even made it to Vabre. Pierre and Marion moved to Cahors, where he took on a formidable enemy fresh from the Russian front—the Second SS Panzer Division, known as Das Reich—who were moving north to support the German army in Normandy. For the first time since 1940, German forces were present on the ground in France on a colossal scale. Pierre and the resistance fighters subjected Das Reich to a series of ambushes and assassinations, which took the Germans by complete surprise. Broken-down tanks and assault rifles littered the road from Montauban to the Corrèze valley. But sabotage came at a high price. In revenge, Das Reich massacred 642 villagers, including 205 children, in Oradour-sur-Glane. The women and children were locked in the church, which was then burned to the ground. Among the victims were seven Jews who had been hiding in the village.

The battle in and around Cahors was fierce. Wounded Maquis were hidden in the basement of the hospital as the staff were frightened that the Germans would shoot the men in their beds. Doctors and nurses also went to forest hideouts to treat the wounded where they had fallen. There were still plenty of people who would happily shop the Resistance to the Germans. After they arrived in Cahors, Marion had a narrow escape when a barman told the Germans she was suspicious. It was the moment to leave and cross France to find Huguette. It was six months since she had left her in Val d'Isère. Once again, Marion was on her own and in danger. At one point on the journey, German soldiers offered her a lift. She wisely refused. She found out later in the day that the SS were picking up young girls to rape them. They took them to a nearby castle. After the girls had been gang-raped, the soldiers threw them from the castle walls into a ravine. Where that was, she never said.

In Val d'Isère, the war was also raging. The Maquis were in all-out combat with the Germans and constantly on the move. The villagers lived in fear of German reprisals. German tanks were moving up on the Maurienne side of the Col de l'Isèran. It was probably just after Marion left with Huguette that the Gestapo chief in Bourg-Saint-Maurice arrived in Val d'Isère with a picture of Hitler that he hung in the town hall. He demanded a meeting with the mayor and the priest. He then ordered an inspection of the hotels. Just moments before, arms hidden in the Hôtel Parisien had been thrown into the Isère River. Once again, Marion and Huguette had had a lucky escape.

The return journey with Huguette must have been equally as dangerous. The Allies had landed in Provence on August 15 and were rapidly moving northward. The two sisters arrived in Toulouse just before sporadic fighting broke out in the city. Ravanel had ordered all the local resistance movements into Toulouse. Barricades went up in the streets. The German army blew up the telephone exchange and set fire to the Gestapo headquarters. Huge explosions echoed across the city as the ammunition stores were destroyed. Gunshots could be heard everywhere and there was fierce fighting at the railway station. Trucks and cars burned as the Germans made a hasty retreat to the north. By Sunday, August 21, 6,000 *maquisards* had taken control of the city and 30,000 people gathered in the Place du Capitole to hear Ravanel speak.

Now pregnant and exhausted, Marion was forced to rest before she and Pierre could return to Paris. She was furious that they were delayed from getting there, as they missed out on the allocation of the best of the apartments of former collaborators that were given to Resistance leaders. It irritated her all her life that they arrived too late for a flat on the Champs de Mars with a direct view of the Eiffel Tower. At the end of August, Schlumberger left Toulouse for London. He then parachuted into Holland to organise sabotage attacks on railway and telephone lines. It was there that he was killed by a ricocheting bullet from his own gun.

Although in 1962, Pierre was made a Chevalier de la Légion d'Honneur, France's highest honour, Marion and Pierre were sidelined. De Gaulle did not accept the true story of the Resistance. The BCRA had been alarmed by Schlumberger's embrace of the entire Resistance, which included large numbers of communists and Spanish Republicans, who were backed up by widespread popular support in the Toulouse area. De Gaulle was frightened that a communist insurrection was about to take place in Toulouse. Determined to restore the supremacy of the army and the civil service, he decided to push Ravanel and his men to one side. Not long after, Pierre, Marion, and Huguette returned to Paris. In mid-September 1944, de Gaulle set off on a tour of France, in which his visit to Toulouse was the most acrimonious stop. After the trip, the story of the Maquis de Vabre slipped into the shadows of history. At the airport, de Gaulle reprimanded Ravanel for wearing the Croix de la Libération, a medal awarded to members of the military and civilians who had played an outstanding role in liberating French territory. When the resistance fighters lined up to meet their hero in the *préfecture*, de Gaulle did not thank them for their service, but instead belittled their contribution by asking each one for his military rank. He then informed Ravanel that the Resistance would have no role in the reconstruction. Ravanel later wrote in his memoirs that he was "stunned" by de Gaulle's attitude. "Our meeting lasted an hour. He asked me no questions. I discovered the existence of an immense abyss between this man who had lived all the war out of France, and the domestic Resistance, which was the vehicle of an entirely different experience." De Gaulle's Resistance myth undermined what the few had actually done, and it left little room for those who had risked their lives during the occupation to speak the truth. Ravanel was severely injured in a car crash in Paris in September 1944 that many considered suspicious. Once recovered, he returned to the army.

⚜

Unlike Val d'Isère, where the wartime divisions cut deep into the fabric of the village, in Vabre, villagers were united in their opposition to Vichy, and after the liberation they remained so. They did not forget the past and remain immensely proud of what they did. From the first anniversary of the liberation, the locals celebrated the story of how Protestants and Jews took on the Nazis. Michel Cals thinks Vabre's unique story deserves to be heard more widely. "It is a lesson in morality and that you must help those in need," he says. The spirit of Vabre's resistance has also left its mark on France.

Catherine Vieu-Charier was born and brought up in Vabre. The moment she walks into the café, I am struck by the Hebrew tattoo on her wrist. It is the name of her late partner, Henri Malberg, a well-known Parisian politician. In 1942, he and his family escaped capture in the Vél d'Hiv roundup in Paris but were later interned by the Vichy government.

For twenty years, Vieu-Charier was the headmistress of the Ecole maternelle des Couronnes in Belleville. In 1995, she and Malberg, both communist activists, launched a campaign to identify and remember the Jewish children who were deported from the city by placing plaques on the city's schools. "It was a movement that started in Paris, but it spread like an oil stain across all of France, as more and more local groups joined the campaign," she says. One of these plaques is on the wall of Huguette's former school in Nice. "My father worked in the textile industry here in Vabre and had clients in Paris. He always talked to me about the Jewish way of life," she says. "Our family hid Jewish children because they felt it was their duty as human beings to help others in need." As she says this, she turns to Cals and says, "Your family were the same." He nods. He has not mentioned this before. He then adds, "In Vabre, what mattered was helping strangers in need and now it is time we recognised that common background in public, so it is not forgotten. That story must also take its place alongside the celebration of the testosterone story of men with guns."

Their work has already begun to bear fruit. Cals was at the forefront of a campaign to welcome Syrian refugees to Vabre. Just before the 2020 COVID-19 lockdown, the first Syrian family arrived. Two others have since followed. Later that afternoon, Cals dashes off to drive one of the children to the hospital in Castres as she has broken her finger. The message is that it is not enough to simply allow strangers and foreigners to stay in the village, but that they need to be accepted as equals and then integrated into local life. The original Maquis register that lists the names of Protestants and Jews all jumbled up together stands as testament to that.

♣

In November 1944, Huguette turned seventeen and Pierre and Marion were married. In Paris, life was hard. There were shortages of everything and constant power cuts. There was only sawdust to burn in the grate. Huguette lived with them in their new apartment on Avenue Bosquet. Huguette did not return to school and never received her baccalaureate. The three of them spent most evenings huddled around a single candle in the living room. The future was still up in the air. The war was not yet won. Fierce fighting continued in eastern France. Just before the liberation of Auschwitz—in the freezing January of 1945—Marion gave birth to a baby daughter. She was given a classic French name—Sylvie. She had a head of red hair, just as Marion had joked when she had dyed Pierre's hair in Lyon the year before. Sylvie soon had a brother, François, who only discovered he was Jewish when a friend told him. By then, he was fifteen years old.

CHAPTER 18

The Hotel

Throughout the summer of 1945, although she was frightened of crowds, Huguette spent every afternoon standing outside the Hôtel Lutetia on Boulevard Raspail on the Left Bank. She was a petite, pretty teenager, who, as Dr. Pétri had predicted, walked with a slight limp. Every day, she waited patiently underneath the chestnut trees hoping her mother would step down from one of the endless trucks and buses that brought over 500 survivors a day from the Gare d'Orsay station. Huguette was living alone in a studio of a friend who had left the city for a couple of months. Pierre had had enough of her and pushed her out of the nest. Her father did not offer to take her in. She was making her own way in the world learning to be a typist.

In June, Roger Perelman, one of the forty-three survivors of *convoi* 61, arrived in front of the Lutetia. After surviving the sub-camps of Auschwitz, he had made his way home via Odessa and Germany. From Brunswick, he was flown to Le Bourget, then Paris's main airport. Perelman remembered: "When the convoy of buses arrived with their ghostly cargo, the conversation stopped. The survivors passed by a wall of silent sadness." When he stepped through the hotel's revolving door, he was greeted by a blast of white DDT disinfectant powder. Inside he was fed and then given a shirt, jacket, and trousers. He did not linger and soon stepped back out onto the street to start a new life. He would go on to become a well-known pediatrician. As he passed the crowd, he had no idea how to respond to their questions, unable to explain what he had been through. He must have walked right past Huguette, who was too shy to speak to the survivors. Others ran up and grabbed their sleeves, but she simply stood and watched. Perelman left without saying a word. It would be decades before he talked publicly about what he had endured.

As Huguette stood lonely and confused in the busy street, inside the hotel, in the elegant corridor between the restaurant and the bar, the survivors studied notice boards, brought into the hotel from Boulevard Raspail. They were covered in photos left by the families of the missing in their lives "before," smiling at weddings or on holiday. But could the survivors identify any of the faces? Joseph Bialot, a Jew from Belleville, who was just eighteen years old when he was deported to Auschwitz, looked at the pictures in disbelief as "the photos exhibited were of normal people with chubby faces, with hair, and we only recalled empty faces and shaved heads."

Serge Klarsfeld also waited outside the Lutetia hoping his father would return, even though he had smuggled a letter out of Drancy to his son in which he had told him that he was now the head of the family. In his book *Hunting the Truth*, Klarsfeld described the vigil at the Lutetia: "He had promised he would come back. He had promised us he would. After all, he had escaped from two POW camps already. So, I suffered less than other children who suddenly learn that their father is dead. Mine died little by little; but this time he did not return. Later, in May and June 1945, at the Hôtel Lutetia in Paris, where we had gone with his photograph to look for him, our hope gradually faded. In August, I was at a summer camp when my mother wrote to me that a Greek deportee had identified my father, whom he had met in August 1944 in the camp infirmary, where he was terribly thin but still capable of boosting the morale of his fellow patients. At that moment, I realised I would never see my father again. I fled the summer camp and went back to Paris, where I wept in my mother's arms. Several times in my life, I have dreamed that my father came back to us." By late summer 1945, it was clear Edith was not coming home either—but there was no one to comfort Huguette. She returned home to an empty room.

The reality behind the joyous crowds, parading partisans, and flag-waving of the liberation was dark and menacing. There were random executions and an explosion of violence against women accused of collaboration—over 20,000 of whom had their heads shaved. Although there were trials and arrests, the legal reckoning was limited. Some of Vichy's leaders, like Laval and Darnand, were executed, but Pétain escaped the death penalty and was sent into internal exile on the Île de Yeu on the Atlantic coast. Assigning guilt was not that easy. The chief prosecutor at Laval and Pétain's trials was the white-haired judge Général André Mornet, who had served on the denaturalisation commission. He had also worked on the 1940 Statut des Juifs, even if in 1943 he had joined the Resistance. His past was tainted, like that of officials whose opinions changed as the occupation dragged on. Of the 300 policemen posted at Drancy, only ten officers and gendarmes were put on trial. Two were convicted but later pardoned. The atmosphere was far from one that would change Marion's reluctance to discuss what had happened.

♣

Marion was kind and attentive to Huguette, but she had other things to think about now that she was herself a mother. A streak of grim realism ran through her. Marion probably knew by now that her mother was never coming home, but as she had no proof, she left Huguette to work out what had happened on her own. That was exactly what Marion did with the rest of the family over the decades to come. It would take years for a legal certificate, the equivalent of a death certificate, to be issued that confirmed their mother had disappeared "in the direction of Auschwitz." In the summer of 1945, the law had yet to be amended to allow the state to issue such documentation. Even if Marion had tried to talk to her little sister, in 1945 there were no words to describe what had happened. Terms like Holocaust, Shoah, and genocide had yet to be coined or come into widespread use. There was no way to express the horror that had transpired, let alone explain why. In 1945, those who survived the camps were left without any support, so it is hardly surprising that it never entered anyone's head to help the grieving relatives. Today, the Holocaust is a central theme in the history of World War II, but in 1945, Edith was not just yesterday's story—she was a non-story.

As early as the late summer of 1944, even before the liberation of any of the main concentration camps, French newspapers had carried reports of the mass murder of the Jews. It was a story like no other. It was impossible to grasp the magnitude of what had happened, and most people were too preoccupied with their own problems to care. Yet again, people simply looked the other way when something made them uncomfortable. A strange silence descended over the immediate past. State-sponsored persecution of the Jews might have come to an end, but anti-Semitism had not. There were few violent attacks on Jews in France, unlike in Eastern Europe, but there was considerable hostility that was often rooted in social deprivation. In April 1945, disputes over housing shortages in Paris prompted 500 demonstrators to march through the city shouting, "Death to the Jews" and "France for the French." Marion would not have been surprised but it would have sent a chill down her spine. At this point, she and Huguette were stateless, and had only United Nations travel documents to prove who they were. When the Free French Committee for National Liberation debated annulling the denaturalisation laws made under Vichy, there were those who opposed the move. The annulments were not to be automatic or universal and each case was to be reviewed in turn. A 1946 opinion poll found that 37 percent of the French believed that Jews could never be loyal French citizens.

At an official level, the Jewish experience was pushed aside. When de Gaulle was asked to proclaim a new Republic after the fall of Vichy, he refused, saying the Republic had never ceased to exist and that Vichy was "null and void." The Vichy period was placed in parentheses and alongside it, in its own box, was anti-Semitism. The official line from de Gaulle was that all French citizens had suffered equally and that he was supported by the communists and socialists with whom he formed the provisional government. To single out the Jews as a distinct group in the population, who had suffered more than others, went against the basic principle of Republican justice. Although, in September 1944, most of the Jewish bank accounts that the Germans had blocked in 1941 were returned to their rightful owners, there was no coherent strategy of restitution. Unable to prove Edith was dead, Marion could not access her mother's bank account.

Thousands of Jewish businesses had been sold to non-Jews during the war, who were now reluctant to return them. A network of organisations was formed to defend those who had rented or purchased Jewish property during the war. Nor did government assistance for returning deportees differentiate between those who had been deported for resistance or because they were Jewish. All returning deportees were given a one-time grant that was adequate for those who had family to help them. It ignored the fact that for many Jews, that support network had been wiped out, as had their jobs, homes, and property. The situation for nonnaturalised, foreign-born Jews was even worse as they were often ineligible for any assistance.

There was little sympathy for Jewish survivors. Simone Veil was called a "Dirty Jew" by a doctor in a medical examination after she returned home from Auschwitz. It was assumed that if you had survived, you had worked for or slept with the Germans. Veil's sister, who had been deported as a member of the Resistance, was by contrast feted on her return. The deportees were symbols of the national martyrdom, and the resistance fighters, the heroic image of France. As a result, the Jews were subsumed into the general victim narrative and their specific experience went unrecognised. Even in 1956, Alain Resnais's famous documentary film, *Nuit et brouillard*, *Night and Fog*, did not explain the difference between a concentration camp and an extermination camp, blurring the specific experience of the Holocaust, and emphasizing deportation for forced labour and resistance activities. It would not be until forty years later, in 1985, when Claude Lanzmann made *Shoah*, his nine-hour epic film, that the Holocaust was properly addressed in French cinemas. It is not surprising that Huguette thought her mother had been taken as a slave labourer to Buchenwald, which featured in the cinema newsreels.

⚜

In the 15th arrondissement, I decide to take a walk around the block where the Vélodrome d'Hiver once stood. It is a stroll that reveals how Marion's reluctance to talk about the past had much to do with French society's inability and unwillingness to accept responsibility for the destruction of not just her family, but thousands of others as well.

In 1946, a small plaque was put up inside the stadium by families and friends of the victims, and the first private commemorations took place on the anniversary of the July 1943 roundup. The Vélodrome itself went back to entertaining the crowds. In one of its last shows, the artist and showman Salvador Dalí exploded a model of the Eiffel Tower. The building was damaged by a fire in 1959 and then demolished. When the plaque was put up inside the stadium, the national narrative was dominated by the Gaullist myth that Vichy was an aberration and did not represent the French State or people. The Vél d'Hiv was on the list of the charges that the former Vichy Prime Minister Pierre Laval faced in 1945 and for which he was executed in October 1945, but he was not executed as the legitimate former prime minister of France.

As the 1960s drew on, French Jews began to find a voice in the wake of the Eichmann trial. The community was angered by de Gaulle's arms embargo on Israel during the Six Day War in 1967, and alienated by the comments he made criticising their support for Israel and the anti-Semitism it kindled. It was something that infuriated Marion and Pierre, who lost faith in the general they had once idolised. Jewish groups then began to petition the government for an official memorial to be built at the site of the former Vélodrome d'Hiver. Lanzmann's *Shoah* only increased the pressure for recognition of Vichy's crimes. In 1986, a stele was placed in a tiny garden at 8 Boulevard de Grenelle. It is small and innocuous-looking. Most people walk past it without stopping, but the small stone steps that run up to a plaque on the wall symbolise the mountain that the state had begun to climb to overcome the myths of the Gaullist era. The monument reminds us of the horrors of July 1942 but still names the perpetrators as the "Nazi Occupiers." As a result, it did not put an end to the campaign for the Fifth Republic to take responsibility for Vichy's crimes.

President Mitterrand's silence and ambiguity over his own career under the Vichy government only deepened the rift. Eventually, in 1993, Mitterrand agreed that France would introduce a day of commemoration for "Racist and Anti-Semitic Persecution." The nearby Quai de Grenelle was chosen as the spot where a wreath could be laid.

Traffic thunders by as I wait on the kerbside to cross the road. On the other side of the street, in the Place des Martyrs Juifs, a small public garden on the banks of the Seine, there is a monument designed by the Auschwitz survivor Walter Spitzer. The monument in bronze and stone shows a group of people waiting to be deported. It is rather banal, like so many Holocaust memorials. It gives no sense of the fear and sheer panic of the moment. The family await deportation together with a pervading sense of sadness and resignation. It fails to capture the horror, the scuffling, the shots fired, the cries of mothers, and the screams of the children as they are torn from their parents' arms. Nevertheless, this monument matters for what is inscribed on it. The words in single quotation marks in the inscription are crucial: "The French Republic pays homage to the victims of racist and anti-Semitic persecutions and crimes against humanity committed under the de facto authority called the 'Government of the French State' 1940–44. Let us never forget." Mitterrand had made an important step forward, even if he still held to the myth that the perpetrator, even if it was the French government, was not legitimate. The Vichy government was, it tells the reader, not a genuine French government.

It was not until 1995 that newly elected President Jacques Chirac put an end to decades of equivocations over France's wartime role. "These dark hours forever sully our history and are an insult to our past and our traditions," he said. "Yes, the criminal folly of the occupiers was seconded by the French, by the French State."

In front of a small audience, he said, "France, the homeland of the Enlightenment and of the rights of man, a land of welcome and asylum, on that day committed the irreparable," as it had "broken its word, it handed those who were under its protection over to their executioners."

In 2010, the year Marion died, cinemagoers flocked to see two films that told the story of the roundup: *La Rafle* and *Sarah's Key*. The impact that they had on the audience was similar to Steven Spielberg's *Schindler's List* in the English-speaking world. The films made the Holocaust part of a collective memory and encouraged many survivors to tell their stories for the first time. If the two films would have prompted Marion to speak, we will never know. She was dead by the time we gathered around the TV at home to watch both DVDs.

Two years later in 2012, President François Hollande said at the seventieth anniversary that the roundup was committed "in France, by France." In 2017, President Emmanuel Macron went further and condemned historical revisionism, saying, "It was indeed France that organised this." Macron made it clear that the government during the war was the government of France, but it was too late for Marion to hear his words.

Hand in hand with the bitter pill of accepting guilt, a movement for recognition of those non-Jews who had stepped forward to help Jews took off in France during the 1980s. It coincided with an interest in hearing the eyewitness accounts of survivors. Until then, relatively few French had been recognised as Righteous Among Nations. France, after Poland and the Netherlands, now has the third highest number of Righteous, a figure that currently includes over 4,000 people. During his historic 1995 speech, President Chirac recognised the Righteous Among Nations as new national heroes. In 2000, July 16 became a day "of commemoration of racist and anti-Semitic crimes committed by the French State and of tribute to the 'Righteous' of France." In January 2007, a plaque was placed in the crypt of the Pantheon in "Homage of the Nation to the Righteous of France." As applications must be generated by survivors, the figure will never reflect the true number of people who helped Jews. There were many survivors who could not revisit the dark years and many who died before the commission's work began in the 1960s.

The Righteous now began to play a unifying role in French society, much as the myth of the nations of resisters had done after the war.

※

In the summer of 1947, Johannes took Huguette to the banks of the Seine in the Parisian suburb of Vanves, where he was then living. He threw the Iron Cross he had been awarded during World War I into its muddy waters. It was the moment he cut his ties with Europe. Betrayed by his homeland and by France, he reinvented himself for the third time.

In September, fourteen years after he had refused to listen to Edith when she had argued that they should start a new life in the United States, he boarded the SS *Sobieski* in Cannes. I can imagine Edith taking a sharp intake of breath, much as Marion did when surprised, if she had found out. The liner was bound for New York. Johannes listed his occupation as a stockbroker. In his suitcase was Edith's silver coffee set.

Once he arrived in the United States, Johannes, who had become Jean-Pierre in France, renamed himself John Paul. He settled in Eureka, in northern California, with Lucette, who became his second wife. She changed her name to Colette and took a job in a hat shop. California was the furthest place from Europe that could offer him a new life. It was also the furthest place in America from his brother Ernst in New York, with whom he soon stopped communicating. Ernst had made a success of his life in America and lived in a smart apartment in New York. Johannes had been left with nothing. He managed to save enough money to buy Huguette a ticket so she could join him in California, although once there, he left her to make her own way in the world.

In 1948, Huguette started a new life in San Francisco. She loved hiking, and on a group hike met Jim Carleton. He was forty and worked for the Standard Oil Company as an economic analyst. He was not Jewish. They married and in 1951 had a son named Norman. After the baby was born, Johannes wrote to his daughter that Colette was saving for a fur coat that he could not afford to buy her. He had just got a job as a barman. Eventually, Colette and Johannes moved to San Francisco, where she worked as an Avon lady, selling cosmetics. The invisible Jew of wartime Paris spent the rest of his life working as a barman in a private club called the Olympic and successfully trading shares in his spare time. Huguette says he liked to chat with people and ask them about their lives, but I suspect that he never talked to people about his own.

Marion and Pierre began to build a successful business making bathing suits, but their marriage did not last. They divorced in 1947. Marion said that they were too young and had been thrown together by the war. Maybe they had simply spent far too long apart, and in those long, lonely months, Marion had become an independent woman with her own mind. Her cousin, Renate, the daughter of her aunt Lili, wrote to Huguette that she felt Marion was bitter and bored by her life as a housewife. She added that she thought her family arrangements were not working out. In what for the time was a very modern arrangement, Marion and Pierre continued to live together for over a decade. In 1961, she moved to London to marry Joe Judah, the man who would become my father-in-law.

They had met in 1947 just after he was decommissioned from the British army. He was proud of being Jewish, and his Sephardi family had built synagogues in Beirut, Calcutta, and Shanghai. Marion never went to synagogue, but she kept the High Holidays at home. Huguette was exactly the same in later life.

In London, Marion spent a lot of time with her aunt Wally and her uncle Herbert, often stopping for coffee and cake at the German

Huguette, right, on the beach with her grandmother Henrietta in California, c. 1950.

Jewish delicatessen Panzers in St. John's Wood. Her grandmother Henriette, Edith's mother, eventually made her way from Sweden to California to be close to her daughter Lili. There is a photograph of Huguette on the beach with Henriette. Huguette is in a bikini, but her grandmother is dressed in an outfit that looks as if she has just stepped out of the nineteenth century.

She wrote to Huguette in English as her granddaughter no longer spoke German, but always signed herself as Oma, *grandma* in German. Neither she nor Lili spoke about the past. Henriette was simply grateful for what she had left. It was now impossible to re-create that tight family network that had existed in Berlin. They wrote to each other, but letters took weeks to arrive. It was too expensive to make long-distance calls, and crossing the Atlantic was pricey and time consuming. Propeller planes had to make stops to refuel, and in the 1950s the journey took nineteen hours.

It was only when he was six years old that my husband asked his parents why he only had one grandmother. Marion had no idea what to say to him. It is a moment that is etched into his memory. Marion left it to his father to explain to him what had happened.

CHAPTER 19

Sunday Morning in Val d'Isère

Almost three years to the day after I promised Huguette that I would find the Pétri family, in August 2022, I meet Christel and her older sister and brother in the restaurant run by the descendants of the former mayor of Val d'Isère, Nicolas Bazile. Their younger sister Stephanie had died a few months earlier. Gathered around the table are their partners, children, grandchildren, and great-grandchildren; Huguette's son, Norman, and his partner; my husband; two of our five children; and Roby Joffo. I have been so consumed in discovering Marion and Huguette's story that this is the first moment that I realise the tremendous impact it can have on a family to have your father or grandfather recognised as Righteous Among Nations. By having made the case for Dr. Pétri to be recognised as Righteous, we have not simply just said thank you. The family has an inheritance to be proud of. Dr. Pétri's bravery, and that of his mother and sister, will be honoured at a ceremony the following day.

Over a convivial dinner, family tales emerge that echo back through the story that I have pieced together about Marion and Huguette. Christel's brother-in-law tells me that his father escaped from a German prisoner of war camp and made his way to England where he joined de Gaulle's Free French. The conversation then moves on to the Val d'Isère they knew as children. Joffo explains that his family eventually bought the hair salon where his father and uncle worked during the war. They knocked it down and built a hotel. The problem was that there were so many family members who wanted to spend the holidays in Val d'Isère that it never made any money. They sold it and built their own apartment block. After Christel's mother died, there was simply not enough room in it for their growing families, so they too built their own block of flats in its place. Suddenly Val d'Isère does not seem so soulless anymore.

The following morning the main street in Val d'Isère is cordoned off. At the Place Frédéric Pétri roundabout, close to where his chalet once stood, is a table draped in an Israeli flag. On display is the Righteous Among Nations medal and certificate that will be presented at the ceremony. It is the highest civilian honour given by the state of Israel. Rows of chairs are laid out in front of the podium. A large crowd has gathered. Bemused tourists stop to watch.

Val d'Isère has a new mayor, Patrick Martin, who opens the ceremony by saying that "Dr. Frédéric Pétri is an example to every one of us." Josef Banon, the regional representative of the French Committee of Yad Vashem, spells out the important role that the Righteous Among Nations, *Les Justes parmi les nations*, play in Holocaust remembrance: "The uniquely courageous acts of this army of the heart with their arms open shows us that heroes are not only to found on the battlefield. There were people who risked their lives but asked for nothing in return, who resisted and held out a hand to the persecuted. They helped to save the honour of France by applying

Dr. Pétri, his mother, and an unknown woman, c. 1940s.

the word *fraternité* in the most profound way." Of Dr. Pétri, he says, "He defied the danger. The only voice he listened to was that of his own conscience. In the darkest hours of the Nazi occupation, he was a man who knew how to say 'no' to hate and barbarity." It shows that ordinary people can stand up to totalitarian regimes. That is the key thing about the Righteous. They came from all walks of life and included a princess, peasants, priests, and prostitutes. Almost 28,000 people across the world have been given the honour, 4,000 of them in France. Trees are no longer planted on the Avenue of the Righteous at Yad Vashem in Jerusalem, as there is no space left, but Dr. Pétri's name will be engraved on the Wall of Honor in the

Garden of the Righteous. Like Pétri, the people whose names are already there made snap decisions that involved a heavy burden of responsibility and that had long-term reverberations. Everything they did was done in secret. It imposed on them a silence that many of them took to the grave. All they had in common was that they saw Jews as people.

Banon invites the mayor to join the network of Villes et Villages des Justes, which was set up in 2012. Val d'Isère and Vabre will be linked forever. When the children return to school in September, they will be taught Dr. Pétri's story. People like Pétri remind us that the Holocaust was not inevitable and teach young people that they can make a difference. That they have moral choices. It is something that Banon says can give "an everlasting collective memory so that future generations can be forewarned of intolerance, racism, anti-Semitism, and Holocaust denial. We must stay vigilant," he says. "It is not enough to simply say never again. It must never happen again." He then paraphrases Winston Churchill and says, "It is the memories of the past that will forge the future." The Nazis were not all-powerful, and ordinary people did manage to stand up to them.

History never repeats itself, but it does often rhyme, as Mark Twain once said. Earlier in the year my husband spent almost three months reporting from the front line in Ukraine. In his speech he says, "I saw the bodies in the street in Bucha. I saw bodies piled three deep in the morgue in Kharkiv. I saw thousands of people in flight—again. This is the story today. It is an awful and depressing one. But for sure, just as war and evil have returned to Europe, there will be a new generation of Dr. Pétris whose story will sooner rather than later need to be told."

The ceremony ends with the national anthems of Israel and France, the "Hatikva" and "La Marseillaise." I look down the empty road that leads down the valley to Tignes. I can almost see our nephew Jeremy walking toward us. I realise that he has not been left in a cold and dangerous valley, but in a safe and welcoming place, among friends. It was not how I expected this search to end.

The reception is held in the Maison du Val cultural centre, near the ski lifts. In a side room, surrounded by the paintings of Pétri's daughter Stephanie, is a round table with photographs of Marion and Huguette that we have sent. They are set out collectively with pictures of Dr. Pétri and his family. Among them are the pictures taken in Théoule-sur-Mer in the summer of 1943. A gaggle of elderly ladies come to take a look. They talk about Marion and Huguette as if they knew them. They have taken Marion and Huguette to their hearts. It soon becomes clear that the sisters were always there when a lady with a Zimmer frame introduces herself. She is eighty-one-year-old Danielle Machet. Her parents ran the Hôtel Solaise. On the table is the picture of Marion with the two men we have yet to identify. It was taken outside the hotel. "I am sure she was staying at my parents' hotel," she says. "I was a small child. My father was in the Maquis and hiding out in the mountains. My mother had to do everything by herself. On the first floor of the hotel there were German soldiers, but everyone on the second floor was Jewish."

My eldest daughter, whose middle name is Edith in honour of her great-grandmother, could not come to the ceremony because she was about to give birth. As we say goodbye, Christel takes my hand. She says that she wants me to send her a message as soon as the baby arrives. Dr. Pétri saved Marion from having to take her sister to the hospital, where the chances were that they would both have been arrested. There is an everlasting link between us. The term Righteous Among the Nations, *Chasidei Umot HaOlam* in Hebrew, has ancient roots in the Talmud. When Cain killed his brother Abel, he killed not only his brother, but all his unborn descendants as well. Alois Brunner wanted to do exactly that, but

Dr. Pétri intervened. By saving Huguette and Marion, Dr. Pétri not only helped two young women, but also saved our entire world. He saved the baby—a boy named Elio—that is about to be born.

> *"The Righteous thought they simply had to live through history. In fact, they wrote it."*
>
> —Simone Veil

APPENDIX

The People in the Wagon

From the list of the people on *convoi* 61 that Karen Taieb gave me at the Mémorial de la Shoah, it is possible to identify fifty of the people who more than likely traveled in wagon 13 with Edith to Auschwitz. They came from twelve different countries and the youngest was a six-month-old baby. In some cases, no one has registered their deaths at Yad Vashem, and there is no record of them at the Mémorial de la Shoah in Paris other than that they were on *convoi* 61. Nevertheless, each one of them had a story that is just as important as Edith's. They, too, had families who loved them. They had dreams and aspirations. It seems the right thing to do to make sure they are not forgotten, so here are their names:

Miedzinska, Fanny Born on May 3, 1902, probably in Przedbórz, Poland. Nothing is known about her life.

APPENDIX

Milhaud, Jean Born on June 14, 1926, in Paris, Milhaud was arrested on the Métro on the way to take his baccalaureate. He died two weeks before the liberation of Auschwitz. His parents narrowly avoided deportation and went into hiding. His uncle, Darius Milhaud, later composed the song *The Castle of the Fire*, which was based on a poem by Jean Cassou, about the deportation and extermination of children.

Misraki, Michel Born on December 13, 1897, in Volos, Greece, Misraki was an office worker. Before World War II, he lived in Maisons-Laffitte, in the then-department of Seine-et-Oise. During the war he was in Marseille. He was held in the Les Milles internment camp near Aix-en-Provence. Nothing else is known about his life.

Misul, Alfred Born on April 8, 1877, in Livorno, Italy, Misul was a magazine seller. He was arrested in Nice. Nothing is known about his life.

Modai, Alegra Born on September 11, 1902, in Smyrna, Turkey, now Izmir, Modai was arrested in Nice. He arrived in Drancy on October 3, 1943. Nothing is known about her life.

Moise, Roger Born on March 2, 1906, in Marseille, Moise was an engineer. He was arrested on September 10, 1943, and held at Les Milles internment camp near Marseille. Selected for slave labour, he was transferred to Buchenwald on January 22, 1945.

APPENDIX

Moïsi, Jules Born on July 3, 1902, in Paris, Moïsi was a construction manager. At the ramp he was selected for slave labour. He gave his occupation as tanner in the hope he would be selected to work. He had been arrested on October 20, 1943, in Nice. He was married to Charlotte Tabakman. He survived, and his son, Dominique Moïsi, wrote a book about his life, *Un Juif improbable*. Moïsi believed European integration was the way to overcome the tragedy of the past. He died in 1995.

Molina, Georges Born on November 16, 1881, in Algeria, Molina was a shopkeeper and was married to Louise Bouchara (below). He lived at 52 Boulevard Victor Hugo in Nice and was with his family in the wagon. His murder was registered at Yad Vashem by his great-grandson in 2018.

Molina, Louise Born on January 5, 1890, in Algeria, Molina lived at 52 Boulevard Victor Hugo in Nice and was with her family in the wagon. Her murder was registered at Yad Vashem by her great-grandson in 2018.

Molina, Paulette Estera Born on December 7, 1925, in Marseille, Molina was a student at the Lycée de jeunes filles in Nice and lived at 52 Boulevard Victor Hugo in Nice. She was with her family in wagon 13. Her great-nephew registered her murder at Yad Vashem in 2018.

Monteuk, Jean Born on July 3, 1889, in Marseille. On the deportation list he is described as an employee, but nothing else is known about his life.

APPENDIX

Morel, Erna Born on September 19, 1923, in Krasnik, Poland. Morel had been living in Nice, where she worked as a secretary. Nothing else is known about her life.

Morgenstern, Sekia Born on September 3, 1902, in Kaluszyn, Poland, Morgenstern had been naturalised French and worked as an electrician. He arrived in Drancy on October 16, 1943. He survived the deportation.

Moses, Marcel Born on September 14, 1906, in Bacau, Romania, Marcel was a shop steward. He arrived in Drancy on October 8, 1943. Nothing is known about his life.

Moufflarge, Estelle Born on October 31, 1927, in Saint-Ouen, Moufflarge lived at 89 rue Caulaincourt in Paris. She was a schoolgirl at the Lycée Jules Ferry. She was gassed upon arrival. Her brother, Henri, survived and registered her murder at Yad Vashem.

Muhlstein, Arnold Born on September 27, 1928, in Strasbourg, Muhlstein was living during the war in Périgueux, and then in Nice. The family was denaturalised in 1941. He was deported with his father and mother (below). His uncle registered his murder at Yad Vashem in 1974.

Muhlstein, Bernard Born on August 2, 1899, in Zaklikow, Poland, Muhlstein, a shopkeeper, was arrested in Nice and arrived in

Drancy on October 8, 1943. He was the father of Arnold (above). He had been in the Périgueux in the Dordogne. Under the name of Benzion, he had been granted French citizenship in 1929, but was denaturalised in 1941.

Muhlstein, Mina Born on November 23, 1898, in Krasnik, Poland, she was arrested in Nice and was the wife of Bernard and mother of Arnold (above). She had been granted French citizenship in 1929, but was denaturalised in 1941.

Müller, Edith Born on March 18, 1898, in Berlin, Germany. Mother of Marion and Huguette. She was murdered in Auschwitz in 1943.

Nahmias, Issac Born on June 8, 1906, in the then-Ottoman Rhodes, Nahmias was a businessman. Nothing is known about his life.

Namenwirt, Eva Born on April 28, 1924, in Borgerhout in Antwerp, Belgium, Namenwirt was arrested attempting to cross into Switzerland and taken to Lyon. Her last known address was La Plaine d'Albertville in Savoie. She was with her sister (below). She had six sisters in all. She arrived in  Drancy on October 8, 1943. Nothing more is known about her life.

Namenwirt, Hélène Born on September 20, 1926, in Borgerhout, in Antwerp, Belgium. A student, she was arrested in Lyon with her sister (above).

APPENDIX

Namenwirt, Hersch Born on October 6, 1894, in Wisznice, Poland, he is listed on the deportation documents as a rabbi, but according to the record of his murder at Yad Vashem, he was a diamond cutter and had lived in Antwerp, Belgium. He was the father of Hélène and Eva (above). He was arrested in Lyon. Nothing else is known about his life.

Namenwirt, Riwka Born in April 1893 in Pogorze, Poland, Namenwert (neé Border) was married to Hersch (above) and had seven daughters. She was arrested in Lyon. Nothing else is known about her life.

Namer, Henri Born on August 15, 1914, in then-Ottoman Istanbul, Namer was interned before Drancy in Les Milles internment camp near Aix-en-Provence. Nothing else is known about his life.

Naquet, Cadette Born on September 30, 1917, in Bordeaux, she was a student and was arrested in Nice. She arrived in Drancy on October 23, 1943.

Naquet, Germaine Born on July 28, 1889, in Arcachon, she was the mother of Cadette (above) and wife of Joseph (below). She was arrested in Nice. She arrived in Drancy on October 23, 1943.

Naquet, Joseph Born on July 29, 1875, in Bayonne, Naquet was a hospital administrator and the husband of Germaine (above). He was arrested in Nice and arrived in Drancy on October 23, 1943.

Naquet, Marianne Born on August 21, 1920, in Bayonne, she was a student and was arrested in Nice. Daughter of Joseph (above), she arrived in Drancy on October 23, 1943.

APPENDIX

Nathan, Haim Born on September 30, 1891, in Ottoman, Constantinople. Nathan was a lawyer who lived in Paris. He had been made a French citizen in 1938 but was denaturalised in 1941. He arrived in Drancy on October 13, 1943. Nothing else is known about his life.

Nathan, Hélène Born on December 1, 1920, in Lyon, she lived at 36 rue Vendôme in Lyon. She was deported with her parents, Nissim and Elie Levy. Elie survived. Nothing is known about her life.

Nathan, Michele Born on May 10, 1943, in Lyon, he was a six-month-old baby with his mother, Hélène (see entry above).

Negiar, David Born on January 15, 1892, in Tripoli, Libya, Negiar was a pastry chef. He was arrested in Paris and arrived in Drancy on October 23, 1943. Nothing else is known about his life.

Netter, Fanny Born on June 19, 1892, in Paris, she lived at 57 Avenue Victor Hugo in Paris and arrived in Drancy on October 13, 1943. Wife of Fernand (below). Her murder was registered at Yad Vashem by her sister-in-law in 1987 and again by her grandson in 2000.

Netter, Fernand Born on August 10, 1888, in Epernay, Netter was a gynecologist. He lived at 57 Avenue Victor Hugo in Paris. He arrived in Drancy on October 13, 1943. His

sister-in-law registered his murder at Yad Vashem in 1987, as did his grandson in 2000.

Netter, Jacqueline Born on September 29, 1920, in Paris, Netter was a typist and daughter of Fanny and Fernand (above). Her aunt registered her murder at Yad Vashem in 1987, as did her nephew in 2000.

Neufeld, Dora Born on October 13, 1883, in Oswiecim, Poland, Neufeld was naturalised French. Arrested in Nice, she arrived in Drancy on October 13, 1943. Oswiecim is the Polish name for the town of Auschwitz.

Ney, Sigismund Born on October 9, 1911, in Vienna, Austria, the only thing that is known about Ney is that he was a chemist.

Niego de Toledo, Maurice Born on January 18, 1885, in then Ottoman Adrianople (now Edirne), Niego de Toledo was a businessman. He was arrested in Marseille and taken to the Les Milles internment camp before being transferred to Drancy.

Nordon, Elie Born on September 20, 1883, in Paris, Nordon was an industrialist. He was arrested in Nice. He arrived in Drancy on October 23, 1943.

Nordon, Fanny Born on November 16, 1887, in Paris. Nothing else is known about her life.

APPENDIX

Nordon, René Born on August 18, 1916, in Paris, he was an insurance agent and accountant. He was arrested in Lyon. Nordon was selected to work as a slave labourer and was transferred to Stutthof in October 1944. He was transported to Hailfingen camp in November and then to Vaihingen an der Enz in February 1945, where he died.

Nunes, Guido Born on November 23, 1880, in Livorno, Italy, Nunes was a decorator. He was arrested in Nice and arrived in Drancy on October 3, 1943, the same day as Edith.

Nyul, Désiré Born on August 9, 1890, in Devavanja, Hungary, Nyul had been naturalised as French. A furrier, he was arrested in Nice on October 8, 1943, and arrived in Drancy on October 16. He was married with one child.

Obedia, Isaac Born on November 5, 1891, in Oran, Algeria, Obedia was a worker. He was married to Adira and lived in Marseille. Obedia was arrested by the Gestapo on October 15, 1943, and taken to the Les Milles internment camp. He was gassed upon arrival in Auschwitz. His murder was recorded at Yad Vashem by his son Maxime.

Oppenheimer, Rosa Born on July 31, 1877, in Berlin, Oppenheimer (neé Silberstein) was a German-Jewish art dealer who fled to France in 1935. The spectacular art collection she owned with her husband, Jacob, has been the subject of several high-profile restitution claims. A widow, her husband died in poverty in Nice in 1941. She was arrested in Nice and arrived in Drancy on October 20, 1943.

Orenstein, Arlette Born on March 18, 1939, in Paris, she was arrested in Megève in Haute Savoie with her mother Zysl (below).

Orenstein, Zysl Josette Born on November 18, 1916, in Warsaw, Poland, Orenstein was a secretary. She was arrested in Megève in Haute-Savoie with her sister, parents, and baby Arlette (above). Her murder was registered at Yad Vashem by her sisters in 1982 and 2005.

Ostrowitch, Leon Issac Born on May 13, 1882, in Warsaw, Poland, Ostrowitch, a bag maker, was arrested in Megève in Haute-Savoie. He arrived in Drancy on October 13, 1943.

Outzekhovsky, Henri Born on May 27, 1917, in Paris, Outzekhovsky was a musician. He was arrested in Nice on October 15, 1943, and arrived in Drancy on October 23. He was selected as a slave labourer in Auschwitz and survived the Holocaust. He was single at the time of his arrest.

ACKNOWLEDGMENTS

First and foremost, my thanks go to Huguette and her son, Norman Carleton, for allowing me to tell her story. Marion died in 2010, but if she had not been such a loving and supportive mother-in-law and devoted grandmother, I might not have been motivated to tell the world what a strong and brave woman she was. My equal thanks go to those family members who helped me to tell this story, for the invaluable help and advice they gave me.

Christel Pétri, Cathie Fidler, and Michel Cals not only guided my research, but also offered me and my family hospitality and friendship. I thank Karen Taieb of the Mémorial de la Shoah in Paris for help in fathoming the functioning of the Drancy internment camp, and Daniel Giberstein and his cousin, Linda Rosenblatt, for their help in telling the story of René Bousquet.

This book grew out of the evidence that I helped Huguette put together to submit an application to Yad Vashem to have Dr. Pétri recognised as Righteous Among Nations. A key moment in that process was when Stephen Mulvey, then an editor at BBC News Online, picked up my pitch to write a story about Dr. Pétri, which was then read by people all over the world. When my agent, Deborah Harris, saw the article, she suggested that I write a book about Marion and Huguette. She said it must tell the story of Jews of France, and above all, the Jewish resistance. At the time it seemed a tall order,

ACKNOWLEDGMENTS

but without her encouragement, as a family we would never have known who Granny Marion really was. I also thank Claire Wachtel, at Union Square & Co., for her fine editing skills that finally brought everything together. Also at Union Square & Co., I am grateful to Barbara Berger, executive editor; Christina Stambaugh, managing editor; Elizabeth Mihaltse Lindy, cover designer; Kevin Ullrich, interior designer; Lisa Forde, creative director; and Sandy Noman, production manager, for all their hard work.

AUTHOR'S STORY

My husband, Tim, told me on our first date that his grandmother had been murdered in Auschwitz. I was twenty-three and had not grown up in a Jewish family, but it did not come as a great surprise and our conversation did not linger on it—we had far too many other things to talk about.

Let me explain why I was not surprised when Tim told me his grandmother had been gassed in Auschwitz.

In 1966, my family moved into a duplex row house on a modern estate near Richmond, in the London suburbs. Our next-door neighbour, Mr. Pelzer, often had headaches and had to lie down in a darkened room, and, since the walls were thin, I was sent outside by my mother to play with his son, Jeremy, so that we did not disturb him. My mother explained that Mr. Pelzer was Jewish and had come to Britain from Austria on the Kindertransport. I was intrigued and kept asking questions.

The move to Richmond also ushered another important group of people into my life. My father soon became very close friends with two Polish doctors at the hospital where he now worked. One was Jewish, the other Catholic. They were best of friends and had survived the 1940 Katyn Forest massacre together, and were both married to Auschwitz survivors. They were like my aunts and uncles, and crucially, never stopped talking at top volume about the Nazis, World War II, and Poland.

AUTHOR'S STORY

The wife of the Jewish doctor had lost her first husband and baby in Auschwitz. The wife of the Catholic doctor had been taken to Auschwitz after the Warsaw Uprising of 1944. There, the notorious Dr. Josef Mengele had carried out medical experiments on her and, as a result, she was unable to have children. My father, a gynecologist, operated on her to ease the pain of her scar tissue. He operated on many Jewish patients who had been victims of Dr. Mengele. The young journalist in me was fascinated by the idea that bad doctors could exist, as I was somewhat in awe of my father.

In the 1970s and early '80s, my father was involved in cultural and scientific diplomacy and made frequent visits to Poland, and he often took me with him. Unlike at home, people talked in whispers about what had happened to the Jews, and Kazimierz, the Jewish area in Kraków, was deserted—the doors and windows of the empty houses banged in the wind. These trips left me with a lifelong fascination with Eastern Europe and led me to study international history at the London School of Economics. It was on the student newspaper that I met Tim.

I became a producer and presenter at BBC World Service, based in London. Then, when the Berlin Wall fell, Eastern Europe suddenly opened to reporters. When Tim was offered a string in Bucharest, I happily swapped gathering news secondhand on the desk for being in the thick of it. I then became a stay-at-home mum in a Ceaușescu tower bloc.

In Eastern Europe, the dangers of modern politics are haunted by the past. In Belgrade, in the 1990s, I found myself having to explain to my small children the bloody and genocidal world that their father reported on. Tim has covered the region ever since, and many more wars and conflicts.

In the late '90s, I went back to work and built a career as a travel writer. It began a journey that would lead me to write this book. In

AUTHOR'S STORY

2013, I wrote *Liguria* (Bradt Travel Guides). How this happened is another story, but in writing that book, I stumbled across the story of an illegal immigrant ship overloaded with Holocaust survivors that had set out from the northwestern Italian region of Liguria in 1946 to try to smash through the Royal Navy blockade of the Palestine coast. I wondered who the survivors were, and how they had made their way to Italy. Answering those questions produced another book, *The People on the Beach: Journeys to Freedom After the Holocaust.* For my research, I traveled from Ukraine to Lithuania and then drove the route the survivors had taken out of Europe. Finally, I went to Israel to ask them why they had decided to leave.

I put travel journalism on the back burner and started writing stories about the survivors I met. I then became the in-house historian for an association called the '45 Aid Society, who represent the 732 child Holocaust survivors, and their descendants, who came to the UK after the war. I took down their stories and unraveled the circuitous route that had brought them to Britain—and then for many, led them to the US, Canada, and Israel. Some of the families of the survivors knew their parents' stories in great detail, but many of the survivors had chosen not to talk about the past, leaving their children and grandchildren with a myriad of unanswered questions.

Then in 2019, we went to visit Tim's aunt, Huguette, in San Francisco. She has lived there since the late 1940s, so we do not see her that often. Telephone conversations are impossible as she has always been hard of hearing but is now almost deaf. She had just been run over by a car and broken her leg. Tim decided to seize the moment to ask her in detail about her childhood, parents, and grandparents, in case it was his last chance.

The conversation turned to the first time she had broken her leg, in the winter of 1943, just after her mother had been deported to Auschwitz. I had been helping survivors tell their stories and helping their children and grandchildren to understand details of the past they did not know, but I suddenly realized that Tim and I were no different. We knew the outline but not the details of the story. Huguette also had many unanswered questions. Who had betrayed her mother? What had happened after her arrest? Huguette was still mystified why a young doctor had saved her and hidden her in his house after she had broken her leg. Why did he risk his life and his family's safety to help a total stranger?

I did not like to see Huguette at the end of her life still worrying about what had happened during the autumn of 1943, so I suggested that I could try to find Dr. Pétri's family so she could thank them. I also said I would try to find answers to her other questions.

When I started to look for the doctor's family and to visit the archives, writing a book was the last thing on my mind. I just wanted to help Huguette and to tell the story for the next generation so they would remember it. But after I found Dr. Pétri's daughter, Huguette suggested that we apply to Yad Vashem, the Israeli Holocaust memorial, to have Dr. Pétri recognised as Righteous Among Nations. The detailed evidence they demanded to support the application led me into a contemporary France that was haunted by the legacy of the dark years of 1940 to 1944.

I then realised that this was more than just a family story. Soon after, I wrote a news feature for BBC Online about Huguette and the brave doctor who saved her life, which was read by almost two million people. My agent, Deborah Harris, encouraged me to carry on digging deep into Marion and Huguette's story. I discovered that it was not just in Eastern Europe and the Balkans where stories of the Holocaust and World War II were yet to be told and understood in their entirety—but that one such story had been staring me in the face nearly all my life, right on my own doorstep.

BIBLIOGRAPHY

There is no space to list all the websites, blogs, articles, and papers that I read while researching this book—not to mention the museums I visited and their catalogue guides. Below are the key texts that provided the scaffolding of this book.

I never start a project without my copy of David Cesarani's *Final Solution: The Fate of the Jews 1933–1949* (Macmillan, 2016). This project would never have got off the ground without the extensive research and advocacy of Serge Klarsfeld. Among his books that proved invaluable were *La Shoah en France* (Fayard, 2001); *Vichy-Auschwitz: le rôle de Vichy dans la solution finale de la question juive en France* (Fayard, 1985); *La traque des criminels nazis* (Éditions Tallandier, 2013); and *Les transferts de Juifs de la région de Nice vers le camp de Drancy en vue de leur déportation, 31 août 1942–30 juillet 1944* (Fils et filles des déportés juifs de France, 1993).

The work of Julian Jackson was crucial to my understanding: *The Fall of France: The Nazi Invasion of 1940* (Oxford University Press, 2003); *France: The Dark Years 1940–1944* (Oxford University Press, 2001); *A Certain Idea of France: The Life of Charles de Gaulle* (Allen Lane, 2018); and his remarkable book *France on Trial: The Case of Marshal Pétain* (Belknap, 2023).

Key too were Robert O. Paxton's *Vichy France: Old Guard and New Order 1940–1944* (Knopf, 1972); Jacques Semelin's *The Survival of the Jews in France, 1940–44* (Hurst, 2018); Anny Latour's *La Résistance juive en France (1940–1944)* (Stock, 1970); Jean-Louis Panicacci's *Les Alpes-Maritimes dans la guerre: 1939–1945* (De Borée, 2013); and Tim Grady's *A Deadly Legacy: German Jews and the Great War* (Yale University Press, 2017).

George Wellers's *From Drancy to Auschwitz* (M-Graphics, 2011); Annette Wieviorka and Michel Laffitte's *À L'intérieur du camp de Drancy* (Perrin, 2012); and Roger Perelman's *Une vie de juif sans importance* (Robert Laffont, 2008) were invaluable resources on Drancy.

Claire Zalc's *Denaturalized: How Thousands Lost Their Citizenship and Lives in Vichy France* (Belknap, 2020) brought home to me the importance of the family's denaturalisation in 1943.

On Pierre Haymann's time in London, two books by Bernard O'Connor—*Churchill's Most Secret Airfield: RAF Tempsford* (Amberley, 2010) and *Churchill's School for Saboteurs: Station 17* (Amberley, 2013)—helped me unravel the story in Pierre's file in the archives in Kew. Sonia Purnell's *A Woman of No Importance: The Untold Story of Virginia Hall, World War II's Most Dangerous Spy* (Virago, 2019) and Laurent Douzou's *Lucie Aubrac* (Perrin, 2009) helped me understand the Resistance in Lyon.

I am also thankful for the understanding gained in the following books: Philippe André's *La résistance confisquée? Les délégués militaires du général de Gaulle, de Londres à la Liberation* (Perrin, 2013); Marcel Charvin's *Histoires... de Val d'Isère* (Éditions du CNRS, 1979); Didier Epelbaum's *Alois Brunner: La haine irréductible* (Calmann-Lévy, 1990); Laurent Joly's *L'État contre les juifs: Vichy, les nazis et la persécution antisémite* (Grasset, 2018) and *Dénoncer les juifs sous l'Occupation* (Éditions du CNRS, 2017); George G. Kundahl's *The Riviera at War: World War II on the Côte d'Azur* (I.B. Tauris, 2017); Johanna Lehr's *De l'école au maquis: la Résistance juive en France* (Vendémiaire, 2014); Dominique Lormier's *Les Grandes affaires de la libération 1944–1945*

BIBLIOGRAPHY

(MonPoche, 2019); Léon Poliakov's *L'auberge des musiciens: mémoires* (Mazarine, 1981); Rémy Porte's *1940: Vérités et légendes* (Perrin, 2020); Renée Poznanski's *Jews in France during World War II* (Brandeis University Press, 2001); William L. Shirer's *The Collapse of the Third Republic: An Inquiry into the Fall of France in 1940* (Simon & Schuster, 1969); Anne Sinclair's *La rafle des notables* (Éditions Gallimard, 2020); and Jean-Pierre Richardot's *100 000 morts oubliés: La bataille de France 10 Mai–25 Juin 1940* (Tallandier, 2009).

Yad Vashem's online archives and the websites of the Mémorial de la Shoah and the United States Holocaust Museum were all invaluable.

TOPICS AND QUESTIONS FOR DISCUSSION

1. The first two parts of the book focus on the lives of the Müller family before World War II. As readers, we know what is coming but we are invited by the author to build relationships with the family before tragedy strikes. How does thinking of these characters not simply as victims help to remember such unspeakable tragedy as the Holocaust?

2. A key theme of the book is betrayal. The Müllers are betrayed by both their country and their adopted country. What are the motives of the perpetrators and the collaborators? Is it possible to understand what drives them? What of the complicity of bystanders? How do evocative details, descriptions, and memorable images allow you to feel more fully the betrayal and fear that the family experienced?

3. Huguette was five when she was forced to flee Nazi Germany and seek refuge in Paris. How does the Müller family's experience shed light on the challenges faced by refugees? How does the story show the atrocity and suffering endured by countless children during the Holocaust? How did Huguette's experiences shape her outlook on life and influence her actions after the war? What similarities and differences do you see between the immigration crisis of the 1930s and today?

TOPICS AND QUESTIONS FOR DISCUSSION

4. What can we learn about our world—and ourselves—from Marion and Huguette's story? Would you have taken Huguette to hide in your home, or even have had the courage to warn her that the Nazis would come back to look for her? What do you think you would have done in that situation? Are people like Dr. Pétri truly exceptional, or can we all aspire to such high moral standards?

5. Is Johannes a pragmatist or a coward? He hides from his religion, abandons his wife and daughters, and runs away from France. He is a man who lives three completely different lives. Should he be judged for the choices he made as Marion judged him? Was Marion indeed as the author says more like her father than she cared to admit?

6. Another key theme of *Two Sisters* is love. This is a story of a mother's love for her daughters and the love between two sisters. What are the different strengths and weaknesses of the female characters, and how do relationships shift throughout the book? How are they constrained or liberated by the times they live in? How do events limit their ability to support each other? Which female character do you relate to the most?

7. This is also a story of resistance. Pierre's love for his country and refusal to accept the collaboration of Vichy challenges his love for Marion, who he abandons at the most dangerous point of the war. What drives him as a character? Are you sympathetic to the decisions he has to make? How might you have reacted? Are we only as good as the choices we make?

8. *Two Sisters* is also a story of women's resistance. Why were young Jewish women so well-suited for espionage and courier roles? How did Marion's experiences during the war

change her as a person? Why does Marion choose not to talk about the past? Is it guilt, anger, or habit?

9. Did this book change the way you think about French history? What pressures and motivations may have influenced French officials to collaborate with Nazi occupying forces? How does the past haunt contemporary French politics? What do we remember about the past and what do we choose to forget?

10. This is also a story of intergenerational pain and loss. Do you suspect that the impact of the Holocaust will diminish as the years go by? Will future generations be less affected by their ancestors' experiences?

INDEX

NOTE: Page numbers in *italics* refer to photos.

A

Abwehr, 59
Action française, 26, 60
Afrika Korps, 117
Aktion Mobel (Operation Furniture), 64
Allied Reparations Committee, 15
American Joint Jewish Distribution Committee, 91–92
Amimour, Samy, 143
anti-Semitism
　after war, 198
　in France, 25–26, 30, 31–32, 48, 50–52, 55–56, 67, 133
　in Germany, 31, 32
　Hitler's regime and, 61
　in Resistance, 60
Armée Juive, 90
armistice, 115
Art Nouveau factory, 16–17
Aryanisation, 19
Aspects de la France, 48
Association pour la Mémoire des Enfants Juifs Déportés des Alpes-Maritimes, 124
Aubrac, Lucie, 174
Auschwitz, 1–2, 71, 77, 81, 130, 132, 138–40, 147–50, 152–53, 185
Azoulay (doctor), 173

B

Bag of Marbles, A (Joffo), 175–76
banlieues, 141–42
Banon, Josef, 209, 211
Barbie, Klaus, 87–88, 89, 112, 166
Barraud, Pierre, 100
Barth, Karl, 184
Bataclan nightclub attack, 143
Bauer, Marc, 178
Bazile, Nicolas, 173, 208
BBC, 67–68, 70, 82, 140, 148, 175, 179
BCRA (Bureau Central de Renseignements et d'Action; Central Bureau for Intelligence and Operations), 112, 186–87, 191
Beaune-la-Rolande, 77
Bialot, Joseph, 196
Birkenau, 71, 77, 152, 159
Blackshirts, 97
Bloch, Gilbert, 186
Blue and White, 187–88
Blum, Léon, 30
Bobigny, 114, 142, 148, 149, 150, 153–54
Bolshevik Revolution, 118
Bousquet, René, 76–77, 81–83, 86, 89, 96, 98–101, *99*, 132
Brunner, Alois, 113–15, 117–23, 128, 133–34, 136–38, 140, 142–43, 147, 149, 159–60, 212–13
Buchenwald, 200
Bureau Central de Renseignements et d'Action (BCRA; Central Bureau for Intelligence and Operations), 112, 186–87, 191

C

Cals, Michel, 184–85, 186–87, 192, 193
Carleton, Jim, 205
Carleton, Norman, 11, 205
Castres, 187, *188*

239

INDEX

CFL 10 (Corps Franc de la Libération), 182
Chabert, Marius "Mario," 173
Chaigneau, Jean, 115, 118, 133
Charvin, Marcel, 173
Château de Nice, 106
Chirac, Jacques, 93, 201–2, 203
Churchill, Winston, 66, 113, 211
Citroën armaments factory, 35
Claims Resolution Tribunal, 22–23
Combat, 60
Commission de révision des naturalisations, 46–47, 49–50, 52
Compagnie Marc Haguenau, 182, 186, 187, *188*
Compiègne, 71
convoi 61, *146*, 150–52
Cook, Robert, 184
Corps Franc de la Libération (CFL 10), 182
Crapeaumesnil, battle of, 36–38

D

Dalí, Salvador, 201
Dana, Eliane, 130
Dannecker, Theodor, 61–62, 71, 76
Darnand, Joseph, 52, 66, 180, 197
Das Reich, 189
de Gaulle, Charles, 40–41, 88–89, 112–13, 178, 181, 186, 188, 191–92, 199, 201
de Pellepoix, Louis Darquier, 29–30
de Rouville, Guy, 181, 184
de Rouville, Odile, 181
denaturalisation, 49, 52–53, 76, 101, 114, 140–41, 199
Détraz, Eloi Joseph, 92
Détraz, Juliette, 92–93. *See also* Giraud, Juliette (née Détraz)
Diebold, Charles, 172
Donati, Angelo, 115
Dormer, Hugh, 88
Drancy, 1, 2, 71, 77, 81, 100, 114, 128, 135–44
Dreyfus, Alfred, 25, 58
Dreyfus affair, 25
Drucker, Abraham, 120, 128
Dubouchage Committee, 133

E

Eichmann, Adolf, 61–62, 69–70, 71, 82–83, 113–14, 140, 149, 201
Eisenhower, Dwight D., 115
Emergency Rescue Committee, 50
État français, 46
Ewselmann, Colette, 130
External Documentation and Counter-Espionage Service (Service de Documentation Extérieure et de Contre-Espionnage), 186–87

F

Fidler, Cathie, 124–25, 129, 130
film industry, 50
food shortages, 54, 98
Forces françaises de l'intérieur, 189
France, map of, x
France for the French (La France aux Français), 26, 46
Frank, Anne, 170
Frank, Otto, 170
Fredj, Jacques, 144
Free French Committee for National Liberation, 199
Free French Forces, 88, 89, 112–13, 157, 182
Free Zone, 47, 49, 82, 87
Freikorps, 15
Frenay, Henri, 60
French Communist Party, 66
Friedmann, Nicole, 130
Frontstalag 153, 40

G

Gamzon, Robert, 182, 187
Gardekorps, 13
Garibaldi, Giuseppe, 94
Geneva Conventions, 181
Gestapo, 167
Ghetto Fighter's House, 124
Gies, Miep, 170
Giraud, Juliette (née Détraz), 84, 90, 92–93
Gonzalez, Bernard, 133
Gorc, Pierre, 184
Great Depression, 19, 25
Griese, Bernhard, *99*

240

INDEX

Gross-Rosen concentration camp, 68
Gruffat, Paul, 93
Grynszpan, Herschel, 32
Guinat, Etan, 90, 92
Guinat, Lili, 90–91, 92
Gunther (Lili's son), 20

H

Haymann, Albert, 58, 111–12, 137, 157–58, 175
Haymann, Pierre
    after D-Day, 189
    capture and escape of, 87, 88
    honour for, 191
    later life of, 205
    Marion and, 57, 89, 182–83
    marriage of, 193
    109th Infantry and, 35, 36–37, 38, 40
    railway sabotage and, 187
    Ravanel and, 188
    in Resistance, 58, 59–60
    return of to France, 180–82, 186
    SOE and, 66
    UK training and, 113, 157, 158, 180
    in United Kingdom, 108–11, 112
Hel, Bernard, 93
Hell of Drancy, The (BBC program), 140
Herzl, Theodor, 25
Hess, Rudolf, 110
Heydrich, Reinhard, 61, 70, 71
Himmler, Heinrich, 100
Hitler, Adolf, 19, 31, 61, 66, 68, 172
Hoffmann, Marcel, 150
Hollande, François, 203
Hôtel de Mont Pourri, 167
Hôtel du Petit-Saint Bernard, 167
Hôtel Excelsior, 117, 119–20, 127–28, 134
Hôtel Glacier, 167
Hôtel Hermitage, 123
Hôtel Lutetia, 195
Hôtel Solaise, 167
Hôtel Terminus, 87–88
Hunting the Truth (Klarsfeld), 196

I

Irène, *106, 107*, 108
Islamic State in Syria, 143

Italy
    occupation of Nice by, 96–97
    unification of, 94

J

J Eichenberg AG, 15, 17, 19–20, 31, 32, 70
Jacob, Monique, 130
Jacob, Simone (later Veil), 95, *96*, 130
Je vous hais (*I Hate You*), 55
Jeremy (nephew), 177, 212
Jochwedson, Ada, 130
Jochwedson, Isabelle, 131
Joffo, Albert, 175–77
Joffo, Henri, 175–77
Joffo, Joseph, 175
Joffo, Roby, 175–77, 208–9
Journal officiel, 53
Judah, Joe, 11, 205–6
Judah, Tim, 26
Judenzählung, 14

K

Kanzlei (Chancellery), 136, 137, 147
Karakaieff, Georges, 119
Kindertransport, 179
Klarsfeld, Arno, 121
Klarsfeld, Beate, 160
Klarsfeld, Serge, 75, 121, 129, 130, 132, 139, 149, 160, 196–97
Knochen, Helmut, 76, 83
Köhnlein, Friedrich, 158–59
konfektion industry, 17, 19, 32
Kouchelevitz-Rosenblum, Lisa, 151
Kristallnacht, 32
Kursk, Battle of, 110

L

La Cagoule, 30, 52, 157
La France aux Français (France for the French), 26, 46
La Rafle (film), 203
La Résistance expliquée à mes petits-enfants (Aubrac), 174
La Symphonie des brigands (film), 31
la terreur, 167
La Virgule (the Comma), 186

INDEX

Lacaune, 185, 186
L'Action française, 29, 48, 157
Landes, Hubert, 185
Lanzmann, Claude, 200, 201
Latalski, Geneviève, 131
Laval, Pierre, 76, 82–83, 86–87, 97, 100–101, 111, 114, 180, 197, 201
Le Chambon-sur-Lignon, 183
Le Corbeau, 121
Le Juif éternel (Der ewige Jude), 56
Le Juif Süss (Jud Süß), 56
Le Pen, Jean-Marie, 48–49
Le Pen, Marine, 49
L'Eclaireur, 48, 98, 129
Légion française des combattants, 52, 66
Lemoine, Antoine, 99
Lettres de Marianne: lettres d'une jeune fille juive sous l'occupation, décembre 1941–septembre 1943, 108
Lévitan department store, 64–65
Libération Sud, 188
Life and Times of Klaus Barbie, The (documentary), 88
L'Opinion du Sud-Est, 48
Louis XIV, 185
Lubetzki, Janine, 131
Lucette (later Colette; Johannes's mistress), 46, 47, 53, 136, 204, 205
Luciani, Madame, 125–27, 170
Luther, Martin, 70

M

Machet, Danielle, 212
Macron, Emmanuel, 203
Malberg, Henri, 192
Maquis/Maquis de Vabre, 167, 181, 183–87, 189–91
Marburger, Jacques, 122–24
Marchand, Edmond, 36–38
Marseille, roundup in, 98–100
Martin, Patrick, 209
Mattis, Germain, 173
Maurras, Charles, 26
Mémorial de la Shoah, 75, 76, 80, 90, 111, 137
Mémorial de la Shoah Drancy, 143
memorial notices, 79–80

Mercier, Michel, 93
Metter, Jane, 178
Milice française, 97, 166, 180–81, 182
Mitterrand, François, 202
Mojaroff, Serge, 119
Molina, Paulette, 131, 150
Montluc prison, 167
Montagne Noire's Trumpeldor (Blue and White), 187–88
Mornet, André, 197
Moulin, Jean, 112, 157
Mouvement de jeunesse sioniste (Young Zionist Movement), 89–90, 123
Mühler, Rolf, 99
Müller, Edith
  assets of, 199
  Auschwitz Memorial post and, 154–56, *155*
  in Cannes, 47–48, 49, 50, 54–55, 56, 66, 67, 69
  capture of, 119–22, 133–34
  childhood and family life of, 15–18
  denaturalisation of, 140–41
  deportation and, 114, 145–53
  at Drancy, 128–29, 136, 137, 138–39
  emigration to France and, 21–22
  family photographs and, 12
  former house of, 124–26, *126*
  German invasion and, 34–35, 39–40
  in Nice, 94, 95–96, 116
  Nice memorial and, 132
  in Paris, 24, 25, 26–27, 29, 31
  in Pau, 45–46
  photographs of, *12, 16, 18, 107, 107, 155*
  roundups and, 81–82
  Wannsee and, 70
Müller, Ernst (uncle), 20, 21, 205
Müller, Georg (grandfather), 13, 21
Müller, Huguette
  academics and, 119
  in Cannes, 47–48, 50, 53, 54–56, 66, 67, 69
  childhood of, 11, 19
  claim submitted by, 22–23
  denaturalisation of, 140–41
  end of war and, 195, 197–98
  family's belongings and, 63–64

INDEX

family's departure from Berlin and, 22
father's abandonment and, 53
former house of, 124–26, *126*, 127
German invasion and, 35, 37, 39
injuries of, 1–3, 167–68
later life of, 205, 206, 207
during later war years, 193
in Lyon, 165–66
memories of, 3–4
mother's capture and deportation and, 119–22, 145, 147, 148
mother's death and, 154
in Nice, 94, 95, 116
in Paris, 26–27, 30, 135–36, 165
in Pau, 45
Pétri and, 6, 170–71
photographs of, *28*, *106*, 107, *107*, 108, *206*
Righteous Among Nations application and, 178
in San Francisco, 11, 75
statelessness of, 199
in Toulouse, 190
on train to Paris, 129–30
in Val d'Isère, 166–67
Müller, Ida, 14, 94–95
Müller, Johannes
  abandonment by, 53
  in Cannes, 47, 51
  conversion of, 20
  denaturalisation of, 140–41
  emigration to France and, 21–22
  emigration to United States by, 204–5
  German invasion and, 35, 37, 39–40
  Huguette and, 135–36, 165
  Marion and, 16
  in Paris, 24–25, 26–27, 31, 60–61, 62–63, 77
  in Pau, 45–46, 47
  photograph of, *13*
  pre-war life of, 19
  World War I and, 12–15
Müller, Marion
  after D-Day, 189–91
  after invasion, 45
  bitterness of, 4–5

in Cannes, 47
childhood of, 11, 15–16
children of, 194
death of, 3, 153
denaturalisation of, 140–41
end of war and, 197–98
family photographs and, 20
family's belongings and, 63–64
father's abandonment and, 53, 63
Hitler's regime and, 19–20
Huguette's arrival in Lyon and, 165–66
Huguette's injury and, 1–2, 167–68
identity card of, 84–85, *86*, 89, 90
later life of, 205–7
in Lyon, 50, 57, 59
marriage of, 193
mother's capture and, 122
in Paris, 26–27, 29, 31
photographs of, *16*, 105–7, *106*, *107*, *176*
Pierre and, 35, 57–58, 88, 182–83
rescue attempt and, 139–40
Resistance and, 81, 85–87, 92
statelessness of, 199
in Toulouse, 190
in Val d'Isère, 166–67, 171–72
war memories of, 173–74
Müller, Rudolph, 20, 68
Müller family tree, 7
Mussolini, Benito, 48, 94, 97, 115, 167

N

Naquet, Marianne, 107–8
National Front, 48–49
National Rally, 49
National Revolution, 49
Nazi-Soviet Pact, 66
Nehama, Huguette, 131–32, 147
Nice Nationaliste, 132
Nuit et brouillard (*Night and Fog*) (documentary), 200
Nuremberg Laws, 31, 94

O

Oberg, Carl, 76
Occupied Zone, 47
109th Infantry, 35–36, 38, 39, 40

Operation Furniture (*Aktion Mobel*), 64
Ophuls, Marcel, 88, 178, 179
Oradour-sur-Glane, 189
Organizzazione per la Vigilanza e la
    Repressione dell'Antifascismo
    (OVRA), 97–98

P

Pearl Harbor, 68
Perelman, Roger, 138, 139, 147, 148, 152,
    153, 195–96
Pétain, Philippe, 40, 46, 51–52, 58–59, 67,
    100, 114, 197
Pétri, Christel, 169–71, 173, 174–75, 177,
    208, 212
Pétri, Frédéric
    background of, 172–73
    British POWs and, 174–75
    description of, 169–70
    family of, 5
    Huguette's focus on, 6
    Huguette's recollection of, 3–4
    Marion and, 2, 167–68
    photographs of, *168, 210*
    resistance network and, 1
    Righteous Among Nations status for,
        178, 208–13
    search for family of, 22
Pétri, Madame, 171
physiognomists, 118–19
Pinto, Oreste, 111, 112
Pithiviers, 77
Politi, Vivette, 131
Pont-Sainte-Maxence, 38
Popular Front, 30
Protocols of the Elders of Zion, The, 30, 118

R

Racial Laws, 94
radicalisation, 143
Radio Londres, 140
Rafle du Vél d'Hiver, 77, *78*
Ravanel, Serge, 188–89, 190, 191–92
Reich Chancellery, 19
resettlement plans, 61–62
Resistance
    de Gaulle and, 112–13, 191–92
    deportees and, 200
    escapees and, 77
    internal rivalries in, 188
    Italians and, 97
    Marion and, 85–87
    memorial ceremony and, 133
    Milice française and, 180–81
    Pierre and, 58, 59–60
    SOE and, 66
    Tsetvery and Szwarc and, 81
    in Val d'Isère, 173, 174
Resnais, Alain, 200
Ribière, Marcel, 133
Righteous Among Nations, 5, 22, 93, 150,
    170–71, 178, 183, 185, 203–4, 208–13
Roi de Camargue (film), 31
Rothschild, Edmond de, 112
Rothschild Hospital, 111–12
Roye, France, 35–36
Rundstedt, Gerd von, 106–7

S

Sache, Berthe Franceline, 92
Saliège, Jules-Géraud, 82, 83
Sarah's Key (film), 203
Schindler's List (film), 203
Schlumberger, Bernard, 180, 181–82, 186,
    187, 188–89, 191
Schramm, 148
Second SS Panzer Division (Das Reich), 189
Selinger, Shlomo, 142
Service de Documentation Extérieure et
    de Contre-Espionnage (External
    Documentation and Counter-
    Espionage Service), 186–87
Service d'ordre légionnaire (SOL), 66–67
Service du travail obligatoire (STO), 112–13
Shoah (documentary), 200, 201
Sicily, Allies landing in, 114–15
Singapore, fall of, 70–71
Singer, Yvonne, 128
Six Day War, 201
Sixième, 89–90, 123, 184
SNCF, 150–51
Sobibor extermination camp, 100–101

INDEX

SOE (Special Operations Executive), 66, 87, 88, 109, 113, 157, 180
SOL (Service d'ordre légionnaire), 66–67
Somme, First Battle of the, 14, 15
Sons and Daughters of Jewish Deportees from France, 132
Sorrow and the Pity, The (documentary), 178
Southon, Alfred, 174–75
Soviet Union, invasion of, 66, 68, 112
Spartacists, 14–15
Spatzierer, Fanny, 131
Special Operations Executive (SOE), 66, 87, 88, 109, 113, 157, 180
Special Training School 6, 113
Spielberg, Steven, 203
Spitzer, Walter, 201
Stalingrad, 96, 98, 100
Statut des Juifs, 50–52, 197
Stavisky, Alexandre, 29
Steinlauf, Germaine, 131
STO (Service du travail obligatoire), 112–13
Sudetenland, 31
suicides, 94–95, 138
Szwarc, Jacques, 80, 81, 90
Szwarc, Joseph, 80, *80*, 81, 90
Szwarc, Paul, 79–80, *80*, 81, 89

T

Taieb, Karen, 137–38, 146–47, 149, 153
Tami (Lili's daughter), 17
Tchaï, Tela, 45
Tel Hai, 187
Treblinka, 139
Trumpeldor, Joseph, 187
Tsetvery, Leon, 80, 81
Tsetvery, Maurice, 79–80, *80*, 81, 89

U

Une vie de juif sans importance (Perelman), 138
Union Générale des Israélites de France, 89
United States, declaration of war against, 68
United States Holocaust Memorial Museum, 90, 122–23

V

Vabre, 181–82, 183–85, 186, 192–93
Val d'Isère
   author in, 177–78, 208
   description of, 166–67
   German occupation of, 173
   resistance network in, 1
   war in, 190
Veil, Simone (née Jacob), 95, *96*, 130, 132, 133, 147–48, 200, 213
Vél d'Hiv, 141–42, 200–201, 203
Versailles, Treaty of, 172
Vichy France, 46, 50–51, 58–59, 134, 199, 201–3
Vieu-Charier, Catherine, 192–93
Villa Lynwood ("Villa of Torture"), 97
Villa Marlier, 70
Village of the Righteous, 185
von Behr, Kurt, 64

W

Wehrmacht's 157th Reserve Division, 167
Weintraub, Jacques, 123–24, 127, 128–29, 133
Weintraub, Lea, 124
Wertheim, Gustav, 15
Wertheim, Henriette, 15, 17–18, 21, 32–33, 70, *206*, 207
Wertheim, Lili, 17–18, *18*, 21, 31, 50
Wertheim, Wally, 15, 17, *18*, 21, 33, 50, 70, 206
White Russians, roundups and, 118–19
Willard, Annie, 131
Willard, Huguette, 131
Wohl, Lilli, 131
World at One, The (BBC radio show), 179

Y

Yad Vashem, 5, 22, 75, 142, 170–71, 185
Young Zionist Movement (Mouvement de jeunesse sioniste), 89–90, 123

Z

Zemmour, Éric, 51

PICTURE CREDITS

Getty Images: Apic/Hulton Archive: 78

Courtesy of Tim Judah: cover, 12, 13, 16, 18, 28, 86, 106, 107, 155, 206

© **Mémorial de la Shoah, Paris, France:** 80, 146, 188, 216, 218, 219, 221, 222, 223, 224

Courtesy of Christel Petri: 168, 210

Courtesy of Rosie Whitehouse: 176

Courtesy of Wikimedia Commons: 96; German Federal Archives: 99